No. 13
Brief Lives
WILLIAM III

Brief Lives

FRONTISPIECE

Portrait of William III by Schaleken

*Reproduced by kind permission of
the Duke of Marlborough*

King William the 3.d
1650 - 1702.

C. SCHALEKEN.

WILLIAM III

By
DAVID OGG

THE MACMILLAN COMPANY
NEW YORK

FIRST PUBLISHED IN THE U.S.A. IN 1956

PRINTED IN GREAT BRITAIN
COLLINS CLEAR-TYPE PRESS: LONDON AND GLASGOW

CONTENTS

* 1 *

A Prince and his Inheritance

FEW THINGS are more subject to changes of fashion than the 'verdict of history' and the posthumous reputation of kings. Royal reputations are created by successive generations of historians; and, as it is easier to win sympathy for a monarch who has fared badly in this process than for one who has fared well, so William's laurels—now sharply contrasted with the blossom of the Stuarts—have fallen into decay, apparently for no better reason than that they were bestowed upon him by the so-called " Whig " historians. Hence a readjustment of values, in which the " Glorious Revolution " is regarded as a drab and inglorious necessity, while the " Deliverer " is supposed, in popular opinion, to have delivered us from something which, viewed in the mellow light of restrospect, now seems brilliant and desirable. Accordingly, the modern biographer of Macaulay's hero is faced with the un- spectacular task of reviving, not the dead, but the inert. This book, which attempts the revaluation of a king, is a plea for the grant of a fresh, though revised lease of that high repute which the royal Dutchman once enjoyed.

Not until he was thirty-eight did William become a king; long before that time his character had been shaped in the iron mould of disillusionment. William Henry of Orange, posthumous and only child of William II was born at The Hague on 4th November, 1650, a point of time at which it seemed likely that the republican and separatist elements in the United Provinces had at last won the day against the monarchist, unifying principle embodied in the House of Orange. The prince's mother was Mary, eldest daughter of Charles I, so the infant united in himself the obstinacy and impenetrability of two dynasties. Nor, in his early years, were there any circumstances likely to mitigate this inheritance; for, in a public sense, William's belated arrival was not generally welcome, while, in a private sense, his custody was disputed by a mother, a grandmother, and a government, each jealous of the others, none of them able to provide that affection which is the strongest influence in the life of a child. The mother, a true Stuart, had the pride and aversion from compromise which characterised her House; while the grandmother, Amalia, Countess of Solms-Braunsfeld, haughty and hardgrained, resented every interference with what she considered her personal prerogative. The Government was represented, after 1652, by John de Witt, the able and masterful grand pensionary of Holland, the province which had distinguished itself by opposition to the Orange princes. Some kind of compromise was eventually achieved, whereby the mother was accorded the largest share in the control of her son. So William started his career with very little experience of family life, and some distrust of those who set up for his guardians.

One of his earliest impressions—at the age of four—may have been of his own disinheritance. In 1654, when the first Anglo-Dutch War came to an end, Cromwell insisted that the peace should be based on the exclusion of the House of Orange from the stad-holdership of Holland and from the office of Captain-general of the United Provinces. This condition was accepted, as the price of peace, by De Witt; and an Act of Exclusion deprived the infant prince of succession to the prerogatives of his ancestors. But events soon showed how vain were the hopes of Cromwell that the English would keep out the House of Stuart, or the Dutch the House of Orange; moreover, De Witt had to face an increasingly strong body of Dutch opinion which resented this injustice to their boy prince.

At this point, it is necessary to allude to the constitution of the federation of seven states known as the United Provinces of the Netherlands, since its peculiar character contributed to William's difficulties, and, later, impeded the co-operation of English and Dutch. The States General exercised supreme authority over the seven provinces, each of which, however, elected its own stadholder, and preserved considerable initiative in public affairs, an initiative which sometimes prejudiced the Dutch in their conduct of war. William's immediate ancestors had been stadholders in five of the seven provinces—to that extent their powers had been considerable, but not complete—and, even thus, their authority had often been challenged, notably by the powerful and wealthy city of Amsterdam. The supreme executive office was that of Captain-general, which centralised military authority; only by appointing someone to that post could the military forces of the states be unified. There were deeper differences. By its wealth, and its large urban population of patrician merchants and burghers, Holland was the strongest partner; hence, its grand pensionary, De Witt, was informally the leader of the confederation. He represented that highly enlightened body of Dutchmen who, abandoning the austerity and literalism of early Calvinism, adopted an attitude of tolerance and even scepticism which provided a suitable milieu for the speculations of Descartes, Spinoza, and (later) Bayle. Dependent for prosperity on peace, or, still more, on neutrality, the Hollanders were averse from military escapades, and so regarded an Orange Captain-general with suspicion. In contrast, the other provinces, as they had fewer misgivings about the rule of a princely House, were less insistent on the somewhat academic republicanism which had distinguished the federation at the time when it achieved independence from Spain. Zealand, a province almost entirely maritime, had long traditions of anti-Spanish warfare; its fishermen and seamen were strict Calvinists to whom the liberalism of the Hollanders was anathema, and for whom war, especially at sea, seemed, not disaster, but opportunity. Moreover, in the landward provinces, where there were considerable Roman Catholic communities and fewer urban centres, the people, less intolerant of another man's yoke, were more likely to acquiesce in the rule of one of the Orange Nassau princes. This cleavage was deepened by events which forced the Dutch, as it forced the English, to accept the principle of hereditary sovereignty. So William had to struggle for supremacy at home, before he fought for kingship abroad.

But, before that cleavage became acute, the character of the prince was shaped in the form which it was to retain throughout life. At the age of 9, he was taken by his mother and grandmother to the university of Leyden, already notable in scholarship as afterwards in science and medicine; but its reputation for learning can have meant little to the child, who probably regarded his university, not as an academic body, but as a memorial, founded by his ancestor William the Silent to commemorate the relief of the city after its long siege. His studies were mainly in mathematics, history and geography, subjects then favoured in the education of men of rank; but he also acquired a wide knowledge of European languages, and, like so many of his fellow countrymen, he became a good linguist. He may well, at this time, have formed his appreciation of pictorial art, in which the Dutch standards were supreme; but books he regarded as no more than means to an end, and men of letters he valued only in so far as they might promote state policy. Otherwise, he was essentially an out-of-doors youth, who found in the pleasures of the chase a preparation for the ardours of the campaign; from early boyhood, indeed, his activities were so dedicated to service, that he appeared to become an institution rather than a personality. This was accentuated even by his creed, for, as a strict Calvinist, he derived from his religion, not so much a sense of piety, as a conviction of destiny and purpose in life.

His studies at Leyden were interrupted in the late spring of 1660 by the arrival of Charles and James Stuart, on their way to an eagerly-awaiting England, after years of impecunious exile; and in the festivities at Breda, the solemn nephew made his first acquaintance with his exuberant uncles. The secure re-establishment of monarchy in England, together with the assumption of personal kingship by Louis XIV at about the same time brought new problems to the Dutch, as well as to their actual and prospective leaders; for it appeared that the days of republicanism were over, and that the future lay with the securely-established dynasties. The death of William's mother late in 1660 brought this matter more clearly into the foreground, since it meant the substitution of Charles II, a facetious fascist, as one of the prince's guardians, a guardian who was anxious that his ward should be

emancipated from the jealous restrictions imposed on
him by Dutch " blockheads." Another, and even
greater royal personage, Charles's cousin Louis, in
the conviction that the United Provinces owed their
independence to French protection, insisted that they
should regard him with grateful subservience, and
that their prince should be freed from Dutch " mag-
gots." So, in the Bourbon-Stuart family circle there
was room for William, provided he adopted " respectable " principles, and kept his republican compatriots
in their place. This was to provide one of the recurrent
patterns in the politics of western Europe for nearly
thirty years.

That pattern was not always obvious. De Witt, now
surrounded by two established kings and a promising
young prince, tried for a time to play them off against
each other, and merely succeeded in staving off disaster.
His immediate problem was the intense commercial
jealousy and enmity between English and Dutch, a
world-wide enmity, for it extended to Greenland, to
North America, to West Africa, to the East Indies;
while, nearer home, it was acute in the North Sea
fishing industry; indeed, it seemed that there was not
room enough in the world for two such maritime
powers. The pensionary therefore sought to strengthen
himself against England by an alliance with France;
and in the second Anglo-Dutch War (1664-67) Louis
and De Witt were arrayed against Charles, a war in
which English and Dutch did practically all the fighting.
In his correspondence with Charles, Louis made it

clear that his enmity was merely nominal—a fact fully appreciated by his allies—while, in his public pronouncements he emphasised how, at great cost, he had kept his word, and helped the Dutch. The conclusion of the war was followed by another alignment of forces, whereby De Witt joined with Charles in the Triple Alliance, which appeared to be directed, in however benevolent a manner, against France. In this regrouping, Charles, it is true, had deserted Louis, and was now associated with heretics; but such bad faith was understandable, even excusable within the family circle, whereas the bad faith of the outsider De Witt was gross ingratitude and treachery. This rankled in the mind of Louis, and provided, if not a diplomatic, at least a psychopathic reason for his intense hatred of the Dutch.

With Charles, the feeling was one of contempt, rather than hatred; and he still clung to the idea that William, if brought up properly, might serve Stuart interests against De Witt. So a state visit was tried. William, who had been declared of age in 1668, came to England in October 1670 as the guest of his uncle, who impressed on the nephew the importance of keeping his prerogatives intact. Then followed a banquet at the Guildhall, and the conferment of an honorary degree by both universities. At Oxford, he met Compton, afterwards to prove such an active promoter of the Revolution, but the most interesting function of the visit must have been the banquet given in his honour by Colbert de Croissy, the French ambassador,

who succeeded in concealing from his guest the enterprise which he had so recently perfected, namely, the
Secret Treaty of Dover. Nevertheless the uncommuni-
cative young prince may have returned to Holland
with a feeling that something very crooked was taking
shape within the family circle.

Events soon dispelled any illusions he may have had
on this score. By the summer of 1672 it was clear that
De Witt's policy of playing Louis off against Charles
was breaking down, and that the two kings were about
to launch a combined offensive against the United
Provinces—not a mere war for the capture of trade—
but a crusade, on behalf of the true faith, to which
Charles had promised both his public adhesion, and,
as far as possible, the return of his heretic subjects.
This gave to William a double importance—as a
relative of one of the aggressors, and as a potential
leader against the other, considerations which induced
De Witt to consent to the prince's temporary appointment as Captain-general. In June the great French
armies crossed the Rhine, and overran the three
provinces of Guelderland, Utrecht and Overyssel,
where, in accordance with Louis's traditional policy,
much time was spent in the besieging of fortresses
which might have been devoted to large-scale conquest.
Meanwhile, the prince, helped by inundations, and
by the defensive measures which De Witt had already
taken, was able to organise the military forces on the
water line, and, so, for the time, the enemy advance
was stemmed. But this did not prevent a sacrifice.

In August the two De Witt brothers were murdered by a pro-Orange mob; and, though responsibility for this cannot be attributed to William, he made no effort to bring the assassins to justice. But the immediate result of the crisis was to raise him to prominence. Before his twenty-second birthday he was confirmed by the States General as Captain and Admiral-general, an event followed by his election as stadholder in five of the seven provinces, and a recognition of his preeminence in the remaining two, Friesland and Groningen, where a cousin acted as stadholder. So the way was at last clear. His youth and a period of military inactivity had served to keep him in obscurity; war and disaster brought him power and responsibility.

By the winter of 1672–73 the first fury of the French onslaught had spent itself, and soon the prince secured the alliance of the Emperor Leopold, the King of Spain, and the elector of Brandenburg, none of them very effective alliances, but, taken together, symptomatic of the fact that opposition to the French aggressor was becoming European rather than religious or dynastic. In George Frederick, Count of Waldeck, the prince had a general who was to prove his worth in this and in later wars. Meanwhile Louis, who had captured Maastricht, failed to take Amsterdam, and in the summer of 1673 he withdrew his armies from Dutch territory. Thereafter, what had been intended as an overwhelming onslaught degenerated into a series of desultory campaigns and sieges, conducted mainly in the Spanish Low Countries and in the Lower Palatinate, a province which was devastated by Turenne in 1674. Charles II withdrew from the contest early in that year, a year in which William distinguished himself in the battle of Seneff (in Hainault) where his opponent was the great Condé. Otherwise the prince's military operations were marked by personal bravery and pertinacity, rather than by brilliance or concrete result—if indeed concrete results could have been achieved in such aimless warfare—while his enemy was concerned more with the spectacular than the strategic. William, obliged to accept the methods imposed by French predominance, soon revealed a certain futility in his operations, which reacted unfavourably on Dutch opinion. As the war dragged out its weary, purposeless length, his countrymen became more critical of their prince's generalship, and so there was a revival of public feeling against the House of Orange.

This coincided with the maintenance of two parallel sets of intrigues, the one as ill-advised as the other. In the belief that he might detach his English uncle from French influence, William sent to London a succession of obscure but pertinacious agents, who did more harm than good; on his side Charles, thinking that he could detach William from his alliances, and cause him to back out of the war, sent flamboyant and overbearing agents, such as Buckingham and Arlington. A way out of this impasse was devised such as could have been conceived only in a period of exceptionally

dishonest diplomacy. The solution was to bring
William more closely into the family circle by his
marriage with Mary, the elder daughter of James,
Duke of York. The motives for this step were various.
Charles was having increasing difficulty with his parliament, which, as it suspected Roman Catholicism and
French influences in high places, was demanding, with
increasing insistence, that the king should range his
country against Louis; accordingly, the marriage might
serve to introduce a suggestion of Protestantism and
even respectability into the family circle. On the
other side, William, now apprehensive about the
decline of his popularity with the Dutch, was aware
that a Stuart alliance would strengthen him against
opposition at home. Charles, while anxious to have
" something to show " to a critical English public,
was busily engaged in overtures for a renewal of the
French subsidy—with all that this financial dependence
implied. At the same time William, equally concerned
about the opinion of his compatriots, wished to go on
fighting, but in the stronger position conferred by
association with a (nominally) Protestant dynasty.
There was another complication. Charles, who detested
his brother, had come to regard him as a national
menace; so he may have had his revenge by imposing
on him an unusually truculent and obstinate son-in-
law. Even with his well-known prescience, the Stuart
monarch could not have foreseen how devastating that
revenge was to prove.

In this atmosphere of duplicity William came to

England, and was married to Mary, then a girl of fifteen, on 4th November, 1677. Statesmen, such as Danby and Temple, both genuinely devoted to the Protestant cause, busied themselves with the diplomatic fruits which seemed likely to result from this union, but the conditions agreed on for a general pacification were rejected by Louis, now well aware of their insincerity, and encouraged by the success of his arms in the earlier months of 1678. Even the House of Commons was made less vociferous by the distribution of French gold; and the public treaty of 31st December, 1677, between Charles and the States General, which conferred a fleeting aura of patriotism on the Stuart monarch, was accompanied by secret assurances to Louis that the treaty was only a bluff. Such were the circumstances in which William married the heiress presumptive to the thrones of England and Scotland. At last, in August 1678, the war came to an end, with the signing of the Treaty of Nimeguen, in which the gains of Louis were incommensurate with French sacrifices and the duration of hostilities. Maestricht was restored to the Dutch, and favourable terms were granted for their trade with France; to that extent, William had succeeded. Still more, he was now marked out as the most formidable opponent of the designs of Louis XIV.

There followed ten uneasy years, nominally of peace, in which England was politically sterilised by the payment of a French subsidy to Charles, resumed spasmodically and less directly in the reign of his successor,

years in which the English navy was allowed to fall
into a state of decay, matched only by the corruption
which spread, like a blight, over many branches of the
central administration. At home, William retained
the tempered allegiance of the Dutch. In Alsace,
Louis was adding to French territories, not by force,
but by chicanery—the chicanery of his " *réunion* "
claims—whereby, among other acquisitions, he obtained Strasbourg. There was no saying what his
next move would be, but it would certainly be backed
by the strongest armies in the world. This situation
was not unlike that of a century earlier, when a similar
menace had been directed against western Europe by
Philip of Spain, and that menace had been thwarted
by the England of Elizabeth and the Netherlands of
William the Silent, but the situation was now more
ambiguous, since Protestant England was now ruled
by a Roman Catholic dynasty in the pay of the
aggressor, and that aggressor was opposed, in Europe,
by both Protestant and Roman Catholic powers including the Pope himself. Nevertheless, so long as
Louis remained quiescent, why should there be any
need for union against him? The conditions were
such as we now describe as " cold war," except that
few realised the necessity of making preparations for
dealing with the situation as soon as it became hot.

To this, the main exception was William of Orange,
and here perhaps is his main claim to statesmanship.
He knew that there can be no satisfying a dictator;
he realised that the apparently dormant volcano of

Versailles might erupt at any moment, and that neigh-
bouring states, such as the United Provinces, were
likely to experience the full effects of the eruption.
In these circumstances it was natural that William,
son of a Stuart and husband of the Stuart heiress presumptive, should direct his attention even more intently
to England, and that he should serve, not as a willing
agent in the policy of peace with dishonour, favoured
by his uncle Charles, but as the European leader
against the system of blackmail and subversion organised by Louis. So, in the decade between 1678 and
1688 William had a watching brief. He was kept fully
informed of events and opinion in Britain by two main
sets of refugees—by those Whigs and republicans who
had managed to escape from the reign of terror which
followed the Rye House Plot, and by those Scots
Presbyterians who had fled from the threats of the
thumb-screw and the scaffold. Indeed, it was from
Scotsmen that William learned the full significance of
Stuart absolutism, applied in a country which, because
of its poverty and comparative absence of political life,
lent itself easily to an experiment in totalitarian rule.
The Prince of Orange could not provide good generalship, but he could provide good leadership; and,
though he had no liking for England, nor any desire
for a crown, he was resolved that England should again
prove the spearhead against the colossus which overshadowed Europe. Any other Protestant state might
have served the purpose; but, because of its resources
and his personal link with its royal family, Britain was

William's obvious choice. It will be said that such a motive served only William and his compatriots, and that, in his calculations, England was no more than a catspaw; but events were soon to show whether this interpretation accorded with the facts. In all this, there was nothing idealist; indeed that word has practically disappeared from the vocabulary of modern historians; there was however something more convincing, namely, the ordinary instinct of self-preservation.

But, standing in the way, were two personages—the Duke of Monmouth, Protestant and popular, his illegitimacy providing the best guarantee that, if he did come to the throne, he would rule with a limited command; and James, Roman Catholic and unpopular, who, into a reign of little more than three years, compressed a maximum of industrious and uninterrupted folly. The first was removed by his execution after defeat at Sedgemoor; the second had to be disposed of by a mixture of force and guile.

* 2 *

The
Leader of a Revolution

THE ENGLAND of 1688 was, and for long remained, an exclusive theocratic state, in which the hereditary privilege and well-being of a minority were sharply contrasted with the precarious existence and low wages of a majority, a state of things which Englishmen could have ended, not by changing their king, but only by changing their God. In order to judge of the more moderate of these two changes, one must keep in view the results which, ultimately and indirectly, can be connected with the English Revolution, for good may come from the doings of men whose avowed self-interest proves to be compatible with the amelioration of other men's lot. Those who did most to effect the changes of 1688 were intent on preserving an exclusive social order in which their religion, property and liberty were safeguarded, but beyond that, they held out no hopes; by contrast, the gulf between promise and achievement is greatest wherever the professions of the leaders are most exalted and apparently disinterested. So the English Revolution was not "idealist." Nor was consistency its characteristic, for many acquiesced in a change of which they did not approve; this is why, in England, it was bloodless, since complete consistency necessarily implies the extermination of dissentients. Accordingly, our Revolution, which might be described as limited or contained, was on the whole benign, and averted a régime which threatened to become malignant.

About the malignant elements in that régime there is room for both opinion and conviction. Opinion will always differ about James II, one of our unfortunate kings, who had few vices and many virtues. In the second Anglo-Dutch War he had brought some distinction on his country and himself by his conduct as an admiral; he had also proved an assiduous naval administrator of a rigorous rather than constructive type. Industry, regularity and piety distinguished him in an age of licentiousness, and served to contrast him with his dissolute but supple brother. His conversion to Roman Catholicism in 1669 was followed by public avowal of his new faith, in spite of the disabilities which that avowal involved; and was more commendable than the crypto-Catholicism in which he might have retained safety and power. But it is almost a truism that evil is often able to make more effective use of virtue than of vice. As a convert, James was anxious to extend to his subjects the spiritual felicity which he himself enjoyed; and, at that time, persuasion was not the only means of attaining this object. These means had been clearly exemplified in the Revocation of the Edict of Nantes (1685), whereby toleration was withdrawn from the French Huguenots. This was ominous because, throughout his reign, James showed an ardent desire to emulate the exploits of his French cousin. Nevertheless, in view of its exalted and even idealist intentions, why was the reign of James so short and disastrous?

Answer may be found in two things—the almost complete eclipse of the King's intellect, attributed by contemporaries to the ravages of a constitutional disease; and the character of his kingship, which, as it permitted initiative, necessitated a measure of intelligence. The first of these incapacities was shown in a certain density or impenetrability, whereby he could shut out from his consciousness those unpleasant things that were obvious to everyone else, a defect which caused him to confide unreservedly in the sycophants and traitors by whom he was surrounded. This quality pursued him even into exile, so that, while plotting for his restoration, the imminence of which he did not doubt until nearly the end, he was thinking, not of a policy which might retrieve him, but of the more rigorous enforcement of a policy that had ruined him. Throughout, he persisted in believing only what he wanted to believe; nor did he show any evidence of concern at the disasters which overtook both his cause and the many who had retained their confidence in him. All this showed an intellectual and moral ossification. However well such a monarch might have fared in other countries, the England of his period, with its high level of political development and intellectual achievement, was no place for such a king, endowed with an unlimited prerogative.

The second of these two matters—the opportunities available for kingship at this time—is more complicated. It was an age of hereditary, absolute kings, anointed with holy oil, and responsible to God alone, a system exemplified not only in the France of Louis XIV, but, to a more moderate extent, in Spain, Sweden and Denmark, where surviving institutions, such as Cortes and Estates, merely concealed the extent of royal autocracy; and, even in Scotland, a medieval survival, the Scottish Estates, provided no more than a screen for the agents of an irresponsible sovereign. Now, all these countries can be described as in a state of normality, in contrast with which England must be considered abnormal. She was abnormal in three main respects; her great common law traditions, which had survived the upheavals of the sixteenth century; her highly-perfected local administration, controlled by an unpaid aristocracy and gentry; and, thirdly, a parliament, in which the old conception of Estates, each limited to its own sphere of activity, had given place to that of a national assembly which, in conjunction with the King, exercised the functions of a law court, a legislature and a council, each supreme, each dominated by those men, whether peers or commoners, to whom alone, as freeholders, were assigned full personal rights. The Civil Wars had successfully vindicated the place of the House of Commons in this system; the Restoration had brought back King and House of Lords; accordingly, by the time of James's accession in 1685, there existed in England—as nowhere else— at least the apparatus of constitutional government. Moreover, this apparatus was based on a very wide foundation—on the services of the unpaid parish officers; on the local administration, directed by the Lord-Lieutenants and their deputies, the sheriffs and the justices of the peace, whereby the countryside was organised for the enforcement of law and order; on the corporations, including the Church, the colleges, the boroughs, in which men worked together for religious, educational or civic purposes. Surmounting the whole edifice was the King in his highest capacity, that is, as King in full Parliament. This was the edifice which James, as King in person, sought to undermine and destroy.

There was the additional complication of James's religion. His Catholicism was unpopular among the great majority of English and Scots, but this was not the cause of his undoing; because, for long, England had tolerated Stuart preference for the Church of Rome, and had remained loyal to a Church of England which often showed more sympathy for Papists than for Dissenters. On this Church Charles II had securely established his power. The symbol of this alliance was the Test Act, a measure intended to secure allegiance to the throne by limitation of office-holding to those who professed adherence, not so much to the doctrines of the Church of England (save by taking the sacrament according to Anglican rites once a year), as abhorrence of certain Roman Catholic doctrines—here indeed was the only theological element in the Test, and it was entirely negative. Still more, this measure had not been initiated by the Churchmen, but by the Commons, who believed that the fabric of English independence could be woven round the strands, however thin, of the nominal Protestantism still embodied in the Established Church. In other words, the Test Act was more political than religious, since it excluded Roman Catholics, because of their presumed allegiance to a foreign power, and Protestant Dissenters because, in effect, they had emancipated themselves from the system of discipline and control maintained by the National Church. It was not religious uniformity that was in question, but national unity, in the face of a threat from Versailles even more than from Rome. Hence, to contemporary England, James's suspension of the Test Act[1] appeared, not an enlightened move in favour of toleration, but the preliminary stage in the demolition not only of the Church of England, but of the Protestantism and freedom of the State.

There is inherent in language a dangerous flexibility by means of which an honourable word can be used in order to conceal an insidious or dishonourable purpose. For James and his advisers the word was toleration, that is, the suspension of all the statutes imposing penalties or disabilities on dissentients, whether Protes-

---

[1] In his Declarations of Indulgence of 1687 and 1688.

tant or Catholic. At first sight, such an intention would seem not insidious, but enlightened and progressive—the main argument of James and his advisers. But toleration, the finest fruit of civilised society, comes from a plant of very slow growth, and contemporaries were naturally suspicious when they saw this desirable object decorating a plant that had sprung up in the night, particularly as a similar plant, flourishing in France, had just (by the Revocation of the Edict of Nantes) been pulled up by the roots. These suspicions must have been increased when an explanation was provided, namely, that as French heretics had long enjoyed complete toleration, they had had full opportunity of seeing the error of their ways, and must come back into the fold; hence, it appeared, the fruit offered so suddenly by James might be as quickly withdrawn, as soon as proselytism and propaganda had done their work. Certain proceedings may have given colour to this belief. By his use of the dispensing power, James had introduced into the administration a number of Roman Catholics entirely disproportionate to their ratio of the population; commissions in the army were given to men of the same faith; the royal councillors included some members of old and loyal Roman Catholic families, such as Lords Powys, Belasyse and Arundel, but (more ominous) two Jesuits, Fathers Petre and Warner. Dominating the administration was the Secretary of State and President of the Council, Lord Sunderland, who, though still a Protestant, was in a process of incubation from which, when the crisis came, a full-fledged Roman Catholic appeared, resplendent in a plumage which was discarded as soon as Protestant feathers were again in vogue. It was Sunderland who convinced James that his proposed annulment of the Test Act and the Habeas Corpus Act could be permanently accomplished by a packed legislature. So Parliament would be retained, but its membership would be strictly regulated.

It was in this process of packing the House of Commons that James penetrated deeply into the foundations of the State. Already, in the last years of his reign, Charles II, with the help of Jeffreys, had obliged many corporations to surrender their charters and submit to re-modelling, intended to exclude all but Loyalists and Anglicans. As the great majority of the House of Commons consisted of burgesses returned by these boroughs, it was hoped that, when a parliament did have to be summoned, it would be loyal and submissive. The result, as shown by James's one and only parliament (May–November 1685) was that, while all the members were loyal, many were not submissive, a fact which encouraged the King and Sunderland to embark on a second remodelling, based on the policy of displacing Anglicans by Dissenters who, it was hoped, in gratitude for toleration and enfranchisement, would comply with the royal demands. Unfortunately, in the process of effecting this second upheaval, the majority of the old landed families, who had long monopolised the unpaid offices, were turned out, and their places were taken by men who had little or nothing of that local prestige which has always meant so much in English life; still worse, these intruders into an almost hereditary preserve were considered renegades, or agents for popery. The result was that James's unwearied activities alienated that large and powerful class which, after the Church, had provided the strongest support of the Stuart dynasty. This does not mean that these men welcomed the Revolution; on the contrary, so strong was their loyalty, that many of them became open or concealed Jacobites; but it meant that most of these families, the " political " families, having been deprived, through no fault of their own, of what they considered their birthright, stood aside in sullen silence when William invaded England in the early winter of 1688–89.

Nor were the municipal corporations the only institutions to experience the onslaught of James and Sunderland. In 1686 the King set up an Ecclesiastical Commission, quite unlike the old Court of High Commission, because vested only with visitatorial powers over ecclesiastical or semi-ecclesiastical persons and institutions. This Commission, headed by Jeffreys, suspended Compton, the Bishop of London, because he had refused to inhibit a London rector who had preached a sermon against the more extreme claims of Roman Catholic propagandists. The same tribunal obliged the University of Cambridge to admit a Roman Catholic, in spite of the fact that he refused the oaths; and, after the expulsion of nearly all the Fellows, James turned Magdalen College, Oxford, into a popish academy. Other institutions, such as Trinity College, Dublin, were ordered to admit unqualified persons, equipped with a royal dispensation; and, at the same time, a number of bishoprics and deaneries were conferred on Catholics or crypto-Catholics. The assiduity and consistency with which this policy was maintained clearly revealed its purpose—that the universities and colleges, even the Church itself, would ultimately be dominated by Roman Catholics. In all this, James was helped by the ambiguity of the law relating to the prerogative, particularly the dispensing power, which he was using, not haphazardly, as his predecessors had done, but consistently and assiduously, with a definite object. This process had gone far by the end of the reign, when it appeared that the Church, the army, the universities, the local adminis-tration, and even Parliament itself would succumb to the caprice of a proselytising convert, encouraged by Louis, and urged on by Jesuits. Can it be wondered at that many Englishmen feared lest their Protestant-ism and, with it, their property and liberty were endangered? Nor were these three things so uncon-nected as might nowadays appear, because at that time, to the non-Catholic world, popery implied poverty, obscurantism and oppression.

Having undermined Church and Parliament, there remained only the law, the institution having the longest record of continuity in England. James dismissed judges who did not obey his behests, and procured from Lord Chief Justice Herbert a declaration that the law is what the King wills. But the judge who gave him best service was George Jeffreys who, after the Bloody Assizes, was appointed Lord Chancellor. Now, it is one of the misfortunes of twentieth-century experience that we have had evidence of massive, highly-organised brutality, perpetrated on some racial or political pretext; and, almost as bad, ingenious and persistent efforts to condone or even justify it. It is consistent with this sinister tradition that Jeffreys is now usually regarded as a stern, but upright judge obliged, in the interests of the State, to administer a harsh law, whatever he may have thought of it; or, alternatively, that he was a " man of his times," no better and no worse than his contemporaries. Characteristic of this, an apparently " moderate " view, are the two arguments, that the numbers actually executed in the Bloody Assizes were less than was formerly supposed, and that the silence of Englishmen at the time shows that no one was shocked. The latter argument can be disposed of at once by the fact that, throughout this period, any criticism of the Government was regarded as seditious libel, and so the public expression of opinion was restrained; even thus, it was freely expressed at the time of the Revolution when it was no longer dangerous to condemn the principles of Stuart rule. Then, as regards the bloodiness of the Bloody Assizes, this is not to be judged merely by the number of executions, but also by other things, such as the savagery of the whippings inflicted on many of the rebels, and the sale of about 800 wretches to the

West Indies for ten years of hard labour, a sale in which the King shared most of the financial profit with his judge. As for the allegation that Jeffreys was really a strict but upright judge, this is disproved by several cases, including that of Alice Lisle, the first victim of the Bloody Assizes, when he showed complete disregard of two things, namely, the principles of evidence, even as understood at that time; and the doubt whether, as the law then stood, a person was guilty of treason for harbouring another not already convicted of treason. Jeffreys had enough knowledge of the law to realise that he had committed several judicial murders, a fact which prompted him, late in 1688, to obtain from James a royal pardon for his crimes. He had committed these crimes in what he considered the interests of two successive Stuart kings, and with the full knowledge and approval of these kings. In order to explain away James, it is first necessary to explain away Jeffreys.

The administration of the law is always the most sensitive index of the conduct of an executive, since it can so easily be perverted by a corrupt Government to remove critics and dissentients, and thereby create that dead uniformity of forced acquiescence so necessary for the dictator. With the help of Sunderland and Jeffreys, it appeared that James was proceeding far in that direction, a fact which, if it did not lead directly to revolution at home, prepared the way for intervention from abroad. The situation, both in England and on the Continent, was closely followed by William, who maintained a regular, if somewhat formal correspondence with his father-in-law, and a more informal correspondence with such men as Compton, Danby, the Earl of Devonshire and Admiral Russell, a group which, as it included what are now called Whigs and Tories,[1] could claim to speak on behalf of something larger than a political party. Neither William nor the States General adhered to the confederacy known as the League of Augsburg, formed in 1686, in order to unite the Emperor, the kings of Spain and Sweden and a number of German princes in a defensive union against Louis, but William was actively engaged in strengthening his external position by negotiations with his uncle, the Elector of Brandenburg; and the existence of the League of Augsburg made it easier for him to obtain as allies most of those who had already joined it. We do not know when the prince first formed the design of invasion, for he was never a communicative person, and such a design would have to be concealed as long as possible, most of all from his compatriots; moreover, he protested, up to the last, that his interest in England was not to dethrone James, but to ensure that the King would rule by a freely-elected parliament. Seldom has there been a more cautious or taciturn revolutionary. Events of the summer of 1688 caused him to believe that his hour of destiny had come.

[1] These terms originally meant Scots Covenanters and Irish robbers respectively. At the time of the Popish Plot (1678) they were applied as terms of abuse; the first to critics of the Court, the second to its defenders.

In April of that year James had issued his second Declaration of Indulgence, with the order that it should be read in all cathedrals and parish churches. The Archbishop of Canterbury, Sancroft, with six bishops, submitted to the King a petition against this requirement; an ominous move, because hitherto the Anglican bishops and clergy had insisted, in their preaching, on the doctrine of Passive Obedience or Non Resistance, which commanded absolute submission even to the unlawful commands of the anointed, divine-right sovereign. The King and his advisers decided on the bold course of indicting the seven bishops for seditious libel, and their trial took place in June, when it was obvious that it was not the bishops that were on trial, but the dispensing power as exercised by James. Their acquittal was a vote of censure on a system of government. This followed a few days after the birth of a son to James and Mary of Modena, afterwards known as the " Old Pretender." The absurdity of the legend that this son was really a suppositious child, introduced in a warming pan, is in itself a proof of the dismay in the minds of many Englishmen, faced with the prospect of a strongly-established and hereditary Roman Catholic dynasty in England; for, while the father was little more than a convert and amateur, the son would eventually be ranged with those Catholic dynasties which had long experience of dealing with religious dissentients. It seemed that some such legend had to be invented, and it served its purpose for years. On the last day

of this month of June Admiral Russell carried to
William the invitation of the seven, including Danby,
Shrewsbury, Devonshire and Compton, with an assurance that, if the prince effected a landing, he would
soon be joined by sufficient men of consequence to
create an army greater than that which James could
put into the field. Nothing was said about kingship;
the professed reason for the invitation was the concern
of the King's subjects about their religion, liberty and
property.

The invitation caused William to press on with his
preparations for invasion, a design which he had successfully concealed from the Dutch and from the
French agent at The Hague. It was known that he
had increased the land and sea forces, but the situation
in Western Europe appeared to justify such a proceeding, since Louis was paying for the upkeep of supple-
mentary forces in England, and in April he had under-
taken to provide for the maintenance of an Anglo-
French squadron. Even more, there was a wide-
spread belief that the English and French kings were
united by an offensive alliance, directed against the
United Provinces, and so the Dutch did not oppose the
prince's defensive measures. As soon as it was realised,
early in September, that William planned to invade
England, Louis offered naval help to James; but the
draft treaty for this purpose was never completed,
possibly because the English king hesitated to commit
himself to active association with a power detested by
his subjects, a hesitation which may have been con-

firmed by Mary of Modena, who resented French
influence at her Court. Moreover, the French offer
was soon withdrawn, because there were not enough
ships in Brest or the Channel ports to warrant the
detachment of a squadron for assistance to James. At
this time, September 1688, the bulk of the French fleet
was still at Toulon.

This fact, the almost complete absence of French
warships in the Channel and North Sea, may well have
proved the decisive factor in the success of William's
invasion. The reasons for this, though not fully established, may be deduced from two incidents, one public,
the other secret, which threatened to transform the
European situation in the late summer of 1688. The
public affair was one of Louis's many quarrels with the
Pope, Innocent XI, but this quarrel seemed likely to
result in war. It arose from the Pope's refusal to
confirm the election of a French nominee, the pluralist
and simoniac Cardinal Fursetenberg, to the electorate
of Cologne. No consideration of strategic or diplomatic importance was involved in this squabble, for
it was a matter of personal prestige, in which Louis
made it clear that, if the Pope did not give way, he
would resort to extreme measures. This probably
meant the seizure of papal territory with the help of
the French fleet in the Mediterranean. The other,
the secret matter, was the private information received
by Louis in the summer that Charles II of Spain was
(at last) really dying. Now, Louis and the Emperor
Leopold were the two claimants, on behalf of their

families, to the Spanish Succession; and, as far back as 1668, they had agreed on a scheme of partition. But meanwhile, here was a chance of seizing the whole. So the French king, having drafted a proclamation requiring all Spanish subjects to recognise the Dauphin as their lawful sovereign, waited impatiently for the death. As his navy was concentrated in the Mediterranean, he would be able to accomplish two things, namely, to inflict public humiliation on the Pope by seizing the papal states, and enforce his claims on the Spanish territories in the Mediterranean. So, on the eve of the English Revolution, the affairs of James and William occupied, for the time being, a subordinate place in the far-reaching calculations of the great monarch.

But Charles of Spain persisted in living; the Pope refused to give way, and meanwhile a third worry added to the sense of frustration and irritation experienced by the French ruler. He claimed some towns and furniture in the Lower Palatinate on behalf of his sister-in-law, a sister of the former elector. The new elector, William of Neuburg, father-in-law of the Emperor, refused either to deliver the furniture or pay compensation, so the wrath of the Eldest Son of the Church rose to fever pitch.

Not England nor Holland, but the unfortunate Lower Palatinate was destined (for the second time in fourteen years) to experience the consequences of that wrath. In the middle of September, Louis sent his armies to the Rhine in order to besiege the imperial fortress of Philippsburg, and afterwards to devastate the Palatinate, a devastation accompanied by atrocities, memorable even in that age. Here was a public demonstration of that righteous indignation which had fallen on the Dutch in 1672, when they had done nothing to deserve it, and now fell, in the winter of 1688-89, on the defenceless inhabitants of the Palatinate, whose two offences were their predominant Protestantism, and the failure of their elector to pay compensation for something to which Louis had no legal right. Now, on any ordinary standards of calculation, the French soldiers employed in hanging peasants and burning their homesteads might have been better employed farther north in the infliction of retribution on the Dutch, whose leader had invaded the country of Louis's only ally; indeed, William feared that the French king would take this, at least a purposeful step. Louis did not do so, and there was thus provided an illustration, not only of the mentality of James's instigator and paymaster, but also of the full implications of the totalitarian state, with all its capricious brutality, a fact which helped to confirm English disquiet regarding the probable consequence of a Bourbon-Stuart absolutism. In this way Louis XIV provided the clearest possible justification of the English Revolution. He also helped indirectly to ensure its success because, with the French fleet in the Mediterranean, and the French armies on the Rhine and later, in the Palatinate, the coast was clear for William of Orange.

Favoured by the Protestant wind, the prince's fleet

set sail, and, after an uncontested voyage, a landing was effected at Torbay on 5th November, 1688. The response was at first lukewarm, for the gentry had in mind the fate of the Monmouth rebels; but soon many of them joined William's standard at Exeter, and they were reinforced by deserters from James's army. The march to London was hardly even opposed, save for a few skirmishes. At Hungerford there was a conference of the prince with James's envoys, headed by Halifax; but the terms offered by William were so humiliating that they could not be accepted by the King, who thereupon resolved on flight. Even before that event, he had witnessed the collapse of the system, to the building of which he had applied such zeal. His fleet, commanded by Dartmouth, after a stormy passage, had done little more than look in at Torbay, to see that the Dutch ships were still there; his army, which contained as many politicians as soldiers, had melted away, taking their equipment with them; his daughter Anne, under the escort of Compton, had fled to Nottingham; his favourite priest, Father Petre, had already gone to France; his best general, Churchill, had deserted to the other side. He was even worse off than King Lear, for his Cordelia was the wife of his chief enemy. In this extremity he turned to Louis as his earthly saviour, and, having first sent his Queen and infant son to France, he succeeded, after one unsuccessful attempt, in landing at a small fishing village near Calais on Christmas Day, 1688. In a proclamation issued shortly afterwards he announced that he had fled from England because of his fear of death.

In his short reign James had applied all his energies to the dismantling of a complicated mechanism; accordingly, his flight was immediately followed by attempts to replace it, a process which occupied the period, known as the Interregnum, between 23rd December, 1688, and 12th February, 1689. Those Lords of Parliament who happened to be in London or Westminster met in their House, though not summoned by a king, and acted in an executive capacity; at the same time, those who had sat in any of Charles II's Houses of Commons were invited to meet at St. James's. These two informal bodies, reinforced by the Lord Mayor, aldermen and councilmen of the city of London, asked the prince to take upon himself the administration, and to issue writs for a parliament. In these proceedings we have an example of restoration, rather than revolution; moreover, as in the Restoration of 1660, the co-operation of the magistracy of London added a certain element of national consent. The elections proceeded quietly, and brought back to Westminster a large proportion of those who had sat in the three opposition parliaments of 1679–81, with the result that the Convention Parliament, which met on 22nd January, 1689, at once busied itself with the work of formulating the conditions to be imposed on James's successor. To many it appeared that the successor would be Mary; but, when William made it clear that he would not consent to act as his wife's gentleman usher, the minority gave way, and accepted the principle of two sovereigns, the supreme regal authority to be in the king. On 12th February Mary arrived from Holland, and on the following day, at Whitehall, the Lords and Commons attended on the prince and princess, when Halifax read to them the Declaration of Rights, afterwards embodied in the Bill of Rights. On William and Mary promising to abide by the terms of the Declaration, Halifax, in the name of the Lords and Commons, made an offer of the crown, and, with their acceptance, the monarchy was restored.

In the weeks before his flight James had helped in this policy of replacement. In the preceding October, he had annulled the High Commission, and had ordered the restoration of those municipal charters that had been forfeited. The death of Jeffreys in the Tower was the surest guarantee that law would be restored. But one part of the mechanism—the Church —proved difficult of replacement; indeed, for a time, it could not be fitted into its place; for, of the Seven Bishops, five refused to take the oaths to William and Mary, so reverting to that rigidity of principle which they seemed to have abandoned in the year before. Still worse, many of the clergy took the oaths, but with mental reservations for James, a practice less commendable than the open schism of those who, because they refused the oaths, were known as the non jurors. So, while the mechanism had been replaced in some kind of fashion, there were parts that did not fit properly; and to many influential men it seemed that the key to their proper adjustment was with the king over the water. That water served to create a mirage, in which the unfortunate James appeared as the lawful king, pining in exile; while, at home, the boorish Dutchman was obviously devoid of that charm and affability which men had come to associate with the Stuart kings. William had won a crown, but not the hearts of his subjects.

* 3 *

The
Parliamentary Sovereign

A^s REVENGE is the usual sequel of revolution, it seemed likely and even natural that, once William had displaced James, punishment would be meted out to those who had shared in the misdeeds of the Stuarts, particularly as there was the recent precedent of the Restoration, when vindictiveness had been shown to both the living and the dead. " Nothing washes away blood but blood " was the expressed opinion of those who wished to repeat the discreditable orgies which had accompanied the reinstatement of Charles II. But—and here is the most significant thing in the Revolution—there was no bloodshed in England, nor did anyone suffer more than a short term of imprisonment for his share in Stuart rule. This was unique. It can be attributed to the initiative of William himself. When it appeared that the Convention Parliament was concerning itself mainly with revenge, he dissolved it (6th February, 1690), and in the succeeding parliament he took upon himself the introduction into the legislature of a royal Act of Grace which, with a few exceptions, provided an indemnity for the past. Some of the persons excepted were not even interfered with; the others experienced only nominal terms of detention. This was so extraordinary as to seem like folly; for many of the Stuart agents were at St. Germains, maintaining communication with Jacobites in England, intent on seizing every opportunity of overthrowing the new dynasty; while, in a manner more insidious, the " collaborators," in office, under a secret " patriotism," were doing all in their power to undermine the new régime. Never did a revolution have such a sequel as this.

Scotland and Ireland were not so fortunate. In both countries there were circumstances accounting for the bloodshed that followed, but (except for Glencoe) it was the bloodshed of the battlefield, not of the block. In Scotland, the great majority welcomed the change, for they had experienced—as Englishmen never had—the true meaning of Stuart policy; accordingly, a convention of Scottish noblemen and commoners, having drawn up a Claim of Right, offered the throne to William and Mary, whose acceptance implied adherence to principles similar to those which had been enunciated in England. The Scottish Estates then abolished Episcopacy and restored the Presbyterian form of church doctrine and worship. William had hoped that a conciliatory policy would be adopted in the North, in order to save the Episcopalian clergy from Jacobitism, but in this he was disappointed, because the old hatreds were too deep. Of these hatreds, the strongest was not religious, but racial. The Highland clans were mainly Roman Catholic, many of them hereditary enemies of the Presbyterian Earl of Argyll; and already these feuds had been exploited by Stuart agents in order to arm the Catholic Celts against the Presbyterian Saxons of the south-west, a policy exemplified in the Highland Host of 1678, when Celtic marauders were used to harry and rob the peasants and small farmers of Galloway and Ayrshire in the hope of goading them into rebellion. The attempt had failed, but the memory of it remained. In 1689 there was again an opportunity of using Celt against Saxon, so James appointed Claverhouse, Viscount Dundee, to command the Highlanders. The clash came in the summer, when Dundee headed a wild rush of the clansmen down the pass of Killie-crankie, sweeping before them the untrained levies of the Government and their leader Hugh Mackay. But Dundee was killed, and, within a few weeks, the Highlanders were defeated at Dunkeld (21st August, 1689) by William Cleland and a body of Cameronians. It was this battle that ended the short war of the Revolution in Scotland, a war in which the Presbyterian Lowlanders succeeded in driving the Celts back to their mountain fastnesses.

In Scotland hatreds last longer than in the south, and the tragedy of the Revolution in the north was one of revenge. Sir John Dalrymple, afterwards Lord Stair, was Secretary for Scotland, and no one had a greater hatred of the clans than he, for the lands of his family in the south-west had been ravaged by the Highland Host. When, by 1st January, 1692, the chief of the Glencoe Macdonalds had failed to take the oaths, the Secretary perceived a chance of using this as a pretext for inflicting such a punishment on the Macdonalds as would terrify the other clans into sub-mission. He expressed satisfaction that such an oppor-tunity had been provided; and contemporaries be-lieved that, even after he had information of the Macdonald chieftain having taken the oaths, he con-cealed this knowledge, so that the opportunity would not be missed. The Massacre of Glencoe (February 1692) was carried out on the instructions of Dalrymple, and can be understood only as an inhuman act of revenge for the injustices that had followed the Stuart policy of arming the Catholic Highlander against the Presbyterian Lowlander. More than half the blood-shed recorded in history is the bloodshed of revenge.

There were similar hatreds in Ireland. Ever since the Rebellion of 1641, the Catholic-Celtic majority had experienced oppression, confiscation and pros-cription, accentuated in Cromwellian times, but some-what alleviated by the policy of the later Stuarts. By a series of legislative measures, including the Irish Act of Settlement (1662) a large area of cultivable land had been acquired by Protestants, whether resident or absentee, and the dispossessed were natur-ally anxious to recover their lands. In James's reign these hopes had been encouraged by the Lord Deputy

Tyrconnel, who filled the army and the corporations with Roman Catholics; and so, by the time of the Revolution, there seemed a good chance that the Protestants would be dispossessed, and old scores wiped off. Hence, the revolution in Ireland began with eviction and terrorism; a large Irish army was speedily brought together, and the Protestants were penned in isolated communities, as in Londonderry. In March 1689 James himself arrived in Kinsale, an event followed by a meeting of the Irish Parliament in Dublin. This, a predominantly Roman Catholic body, annulled the Act of Settlement and those measures which subordinated the country to Westminster; under the personal leadership of their king, who was equipped with French money and French troops, there seemed a reasonable hope that the Irish would shake off their ancient bondage, even if it meant the substitution of Bourbon or Stuart fetters in its place.

There then followed incidents of treachery, fortitude and courage such as could hardly be surpassed in even the most grandiose of epics. The first of these incidents was the 100-days' siege of Londonderry. Had the city fallen, the whole of Ulster would have succumbed, and James's cause in Ireland might well have triumphed. Long delay in bringing help to the distressed city is accounted for by the fact that William had few resources for dealing with such a situation. The English navy, after years of neglect, was deficient in ships and supplies; the army created by James had dispersed; still worse, many of the officials whom the

W.   D

King was obliged to employ were not Jacobites, but
crypto-Jacobites, well able to conceal their treachery
under the guise of administrative service. Of this,
a tragic example was provided in the autumn of 1689,
shortly after the relief of Londonderry. William
rightly judged that James must be expelled from
Ireland; but how? In August, he sent to Ulster the
aged Schomberg, with about 15,000 men, including
Dutch, Danes and Huguenots, equipped, or rather,
not equipped by Henry Shales, who had served as
James's commissary general. James's army was
stationed at Ardee; Schomberg, with his inferior
forces, established himself a few miles farther north at
Dundalk. An unusually wet autumn and early
winter brought privation and disease to men deprived
of the necessary clothing and equipment, with the
result that, in November, their leader retreated to
Belfast, having lost nearly half his men by criminal
neglect. This was the most signal triumph achieved
by those " collaborators " who were secretly serving
the Stuart cause.

These things show how strong were the forces
opposed to the Revolution, and how badly served was
the Deliverer. As a man of action, William decided
that he must intervene in person—the continental
campaigns must wait until the situation in Ireland
was retrieved—so, in the early summer of 1690 he
landed at Carrickfergus with about 30,000 men, and
advanced to contest with James control of the Pale
and of Dublin. On the first day of July 1690 was

fought at the Boyne, near Drogheda, the decisive
battle of this Irish war, when William, with his cosmo-
politan army, defeated and drove off James, with his
array of French, Irish and Jacobites. This was followed
by James's flight back to France, and by the retreat
of his troops to Galway and Limerick. In the following
year at Aughrim, between Athlone and Limerick,
William's Dutch general, Ginkel, defeated the Irish
army under the French leader St. Ruth (12th July,
1691). The capitulation of Limerick later in the same
year completed the military conquest of Ireland.

As William had tried to apply a policy of conciliation
in Scotland, so he hoped to win over the Irish Celts by
compromise and concession. These were the qualities
manifest in the first draft of the Articles of Limerick
which, in a modified form were accepted by the two
opposing generals, Ginkel and Sarsfield. By these
Articles, all who wished to join James's army in France
were free to do so—an extraordinary concession—
while, to those who remained at home, was extended
the same measure of toleration as they had enjoyed
in the reign of Charles II. But these generous terms
were afterwards whittled down, and the English
legislature passed measures for the sister country
which had the effect of destroying the spirit of the
Articles of Limerick. These measures excluded from
office all who refused certain oaths which, without
reserve, solemnly repudiated all that was essentially
Catholic; and, in this way, so far as legislation could
do it, the Celts were treated as helots. This was soon

followed by economic repression. A clothing industry was evolving from Irish wool; but an English Act forbade the export of Irish cloth even to foreign countries. Smuggling could not compensate for the injustice of this prohibition. Accordingly, the Revolution brought little but misfortune to Ireland, and intensified those racial hatreds from which it was England's good fortune to be completely free.

Throughout the greater part of the old empire the Revolution was warmly welcomed; indeed, Massachusetts almost anticipated it, so strong was New England's dislike of James's Roman Catholic agents. It seemed possible that the change of dynasty would be followed by a more active policy against the French in Canada and the West Indies, but the hostilities that ensued were almost completely barren of results. Nevertheless, it is possible that, if the French had been expelled from the mainland, the New England colonies would have broken away altogether, since they were dependent almost entirely on the home country for their defence; and so our military failures in the west helped to preserve a somewhat precarious situation, in which the Empire was regarded primarily as a source of raw material, much of it required for England's re-export trade. Generally therefore, by the year 1692, the situation was that the Revolution had been completed in Great Britain, Ireland and the Plantations, though it was never secure, so long as Louis XIV lived. The story of how it had to be fought for in western Europe belongs to a later chapter; meanwhile, this chapter seeks to summarise the achievement of a settlement at home.

That settlement was characterised by a number of compromises, and even inconsistencies, such as have often impressed foreign observers. Of abstract principle there was scarcely anything; indeed, the only semblance of abstract doctrine—an affirmation of the social contract—was eliminated, in return for acceptance of the highly controversial axiom that, as James had abdicated, the throne was therefore vacant. What mattered to the legislators was not " reform," but the devising of safeguards to ensure that certain evils, fresh in the memory of the nation, should not recur. There were long debates on what James's flight really implied, and on the question of William's status; eventually, a compromise was reached by treating the royal flight as tantamount to abdication, and conferring sovereign powers on both William and Mary. This helped to soothe the scruples of those who, in the belief that James's son was spurious, could regard Mary as her father's lawful successor, a situation which lasted until 1694 when, with the death of Mary, William ruled alone. Meanwhile, there was Mary's younger sister Anne, of whose numerous progeny only the Duke of Gloucester, born in 1689, seemed likely to survive. This possibility caused Parliament to drop the idea of including the Hanoverians in the succession, but the Hanoverian claim was revived and established by the Act of Settlement (1701), when, with the death of the Duke of Gloucester, it seemed certain that neither Anne nor William would have an heir. In these ways, the appearance at least of hereditary right was retained, for it was stipulated that William's heirs should succeed only after failure of heirs to Mary and Anne; accordingly, with the failure of heirs to all three, the succession was vested in the Protestant descendants of James I.

These legislative measures were based on the general axiom, enunciated in the Bill of Rights, that no papist, nor anyone married to a papist should succeed to the throne. The Bill of Rights began with the statement that James, with the help of evil councillors and judges, had attempted to subvert the Protestant religion and the laws and liberties of the kingdom. Some of the methods by which he had tried to effect this object were enumerated, such as his use of the dispensing and suspending power, his raising and keeping a standing army in time of peace without consent of Parliament, his violation of freedom of election of Members of Parliament, the imposing of excessive fines, the demanding of excessive bail and the infliction of illegal and cruel punishments. All these things having been declared illegal, the Act then provided that, for the redress of grievances, Parliament should be summoned frequently; here indeed was the only clear requirement imposed on the sovereign. The effect was that the prerogative remained substantially what it had been under the later Stuarts, for the King retained the right to declare war and make peace, to veto legislation, to pardon offences, and to appoint to

high offices of State, including that of judge. Nevertheless, as well as assuring for the subject certain
elementary rights, such as the right to petition, the
right to moderate bail and the right to trial by juries
of freeholders, the Bill of Rights clearly implies a
contract between king and legislature, and it concludes
with an expression of confidence that William and
Mary would complete the liberation already in-
augurated. Experience had shown how easily the
letter of the law might be kept, while its spirit was
violated, hence the legislators of the Convention Parliament founded parliamentary sovereignty, not on the
narrow ledge of statutory enactment, but on the broad
basis of good faith. William honoured that faith.

As good faith was manifest in the Bill of Rights, so
an element of enlightenment can be traced in another
measure passed by the Convention Parliament, namely,
the Toleration Act. This measure shows how the
enlargement of the rights of the subject has come, not
by sweeping measures of reform, but by the accumulation of piecemeal legislation. Protestant Dissenters
had been heavily penalised by the Clarendon Code of
1664-65, mainly on the ground that, with their
Puritan and Cromwellian associations, they were a
danger to the State; but, in the excitement of the Popish
Plot, there was such anti-Catholic feeling, that a certain
kinship came to be established among Protestant communities, a kinship extended even to the detested
Scottish Presbyterians who, after all, had suffered
most from Stuart rule. At this time, there was no

thought of granting full rights of citizenship to all Protestant Dissenters, but at least there was a recognition that they did not constitute a danger to the established order. Characteristically, therefore, the penal legislation against them was not annulled; but that legislation was no longer to be enforced against those who complied with certain requirements, such as taking the new oaths and making a declaration against transubstantiation, while their pastors were required to profess adherence to certain of the Thirty-nine Articles. Their worship was no longer to be conducted in secret, and in this way, some kind of status, however imperfect, was conferred on Protestant dissent. This state of things lasted until 1828.

Among the urgent problems confronting the Revolution legislators were, first, the necessity of implementing the requirement of the Bill of Rights that Parliament should be held frequently; and second, that the position of the soldier should be legalised. The first of these was secured by the Triennial Act of 1694 which enacted that Parliament should meet at least once every three years, and that its life should not last longer than three years. The longest interval in the succession of six Parliaments summoned by William was ten months (April 1700–February 1701), and the fact that the length of this interval caused criticism is evidence of how the nation was becoming habituated to the regular meeting of Parliament. The limitation of its life was extended to seven years by the Septennial Act of 1716 because it was obvious, even before that date, that the House of Commons had become the most important branch of the legislature; and that, for the full exercise of its powers, it needed a longer duration than that allowed by the Triennial Act. Parliament had come to stay, but only after experiment could there be a clear determination of its duration.

The Mutiny Act had its more remote origin in the necessity of bringing the military forces of the Crown within the terms of the constitution. That, for long, had been the position of the navy and the militia, in so far as their maintenance and discipline were provided for by statute; but, with the army, it was very different. England had never been a military nation; indeed, she prided herself on that fact; and two things had confirmed this tradition—experience of Cromwellian rule and of the fate of those few expeditionary forces that had been sent to the Continent since Henry VIII's time. Moreover, standing armies were anathema to Englishmen, because they might be used (as in Stuart Scotland) for dragooning the countryside; and, when not employed for that purpose, they might, it was thought, debauch a whole neighbourhood. Now, one of the implications of the Revolution was war with France; and it was generally recognised that this would entail, as well as war at sea, engagement in continental campaigns. The majority in the Commons recognising this necessity was not a large one, and, for a time, it had to be propped up by places and pensions; moreover, there was agreement among all parties that a standing army in time of peace was indefensible.

Here again, a compromise was effected, for the Mutiny Act of 1689, at first valid for only six months, was later made annual, and the first series ended with the conclusion of peace in 1697. These Acts had nothing to do with parliamentary grants; collectively, they created a code of military law, imposing the penalty of death on certain offences which had long been treated by the common law as no more than misdemeanours. In order to effect such a transformation, there was needed almost a change of mentality, because hitherto the English soldier, usually a hooligan, had prided himself on the preservation of his civil rights, and so it had often been difficult to induce him to obey the commands of an officer; moreover, he usually thought of himself not as a servant of the State but as a member of a private company. This difficulty had to be overcome by the imposition of a special disciplinary code; here indeed was one of the penalties of the Revolution, that England, having lost her old insularity, had to acquiesce in one of the limitations imposed on the soldier by continental states. But there was this compensation that, contrary to the usual practice of continental armies, many of the new English regiments, as they took shape, were known by something more distinctive than a mere number, for units of the infantry came, more and more, to be designated according to the county or district where they were recruited, a personal association which helped to create a spirit of solidarity and comradeship such as the older system had never achieved.

By these legislative measures, England parted company with the old order; and, as a Protestant, maritime state, advanced towards world supremacy. Of this parting of the ways, the clearest indication was provided by the new coronation oath, imposed by statute, and sworn to by William and Mary at their coronation on 11th April, 1689. It has remained the standard form ever since, except for changes necessitated by the Union with Scotland. Contemporaries attached great importance to this new oath, some indeed regarding it as the essential thing in the Revolution settlement. Why was this so?

Because the new oath, drawn up by laymen, mainly for laymen, was intended to obviate, so far as that could be done by a solemn obligation imposed on the Sovereign, some of the most serious evils experienced under the Stuarts. This fact does not at once emerge clearly from the wording of the formula. As in the past, the King was required to maintain and defend the Church of England; but he had also to swear that he would rule by the statutes of parliament, and that he would uphold " the Protestant Reformed Religion established by law." Of these new obligations the first was clear and non-controversial. The King was no longer the sole lawgiver; thenceforth, he was no more than one of the essential elements in the legislature. His monarchy was hereditary, but also parliamentary.

But the other newcomer is more difficult to understand. Surely, it will be said, the obligation to main-

tain and defend the Church of England was sufficient
guarantee of the nation's Protestantism? But contemporaries did not think so; indeed, the Commons
rejected the proposed amendment, " Protestant Church
of England," possibly because of doubts whether there
existed any such institution. The debates showed that,
in the opinion of a majority, there was needed some
profession of faith, other than, or in addition to, that
implied by support of the Established Church; and so
a curious dual formula was evolved, a formula which
can be accounted for mainly by concern at the ambiguous role played by the church of England throughout
the greater part of Stuart history. To an earlier generation, Laud had typified a romanising tradition in that
Church, enforcing its decrees in Star Chamber and
Court of High Commission; then, under the later
Stuarts, the National Church seemed to have acquiesced
first in the crypto-Catholicism of one king and the
public Catholicism of another. True, there were the
Seven Bishops, but a majority of them refused allegiance to William and Mary, and it was well known
that many of the clergy, still loyal to James, repudiated
the Revolution altogether. Moreover, most of them
would have indignantly rejected the application of the
word " Protestant " to their Church.

In Europe, at the time of the Revolution, there could
be only two camps—Protestant or Reformed, as represented by the Scots, the Dutch, the Swedes and many
of the German princes; and Roman Catholic, as
represented by Louis XIV and the Jesuits. In the

first camp were communities technically classed as Protestant or Reformed, according as they derived their origins from Luther or from Calvin and Zwingli. Protestant and Reformed had at first been fierce enemies but, after The Thirty Years War, their animosities had been greatly mitigated by their common opposition to Rome. Now, the English legislators, unconcerned about these old animosities, were intent on extracting from the sixteenth-century revolts against Rome all that would now serve their purpose against Versailles. By Protestant, they had in mind the changes of Henry VIII's reign, when vast areas of church lands had been acquired by laymen, many of them among the ancestors of those who devised the new oath and still held their estates by the title of these confiscations; the term also implied the complete subordination of Church to State. By Reformed, they meant those changes of Elizabeth's reign whereby, in consequence of association, partly diplomatic or political, with Reformed communities on the Continent, certain Calvinist elements had been admitted into the official doctrine professed in the Thirty-nine Articles, from which they have not yet been removed. These two sets of changes, the Henrician and the Elizabethan had been authorised by law; whereas there was nothing in law to warrant the assumption that the Church of England, however remote its origins, had any affiliation or association with the Church of Rome. The dual phrase had this additional advantage that it excluded the casuist who might argue that, after the

Council of Trent, the Roman Catholic Church was a
" Reformed " Church. Seldom has a pair of words
been made to accommodate so many diverse meanings,
each serving a definite purpose, all of them eloquent
of an almost desperate attempt by laymen to exclude,
in this matter of fundamental importance, every
attempt at chicanery or evasion.

The theology of the legislators may have been
eclectic, but their meaning was clear and emphatic.
They meant that, whatever description might be
applied by the clergy to their Church, England was a
Protestant State, a partner with other Protestant and
Reformed states in the campaign against proselytising,
persecuting Catholicism as represented by Louis XIV.
Still more, their meaning was that the national church
was absolutely subordinate to the State. No longer
would there be an opportunity for an Archbishop Laud
or a Father Petre. Thenceforth there was assured to
the clergy in England a public place, honourable and
responsible, within the limits of their sacred calling,
but the persecuting prelate and the backstairs priest
were now things of the past. Here was the essence,
many may think the justification, of the English
Revolution.

By these legislative measures there was created for
absolutist William, not a carefully regulated constitutional government such as we have to-day, but a
milieu within which he could exercise an initiative
nearly as great as that of his predecessors. The main
consequence was that he acted as his own first minister

if only because there was no ministry; indeed that term is inconceivable without some kind of party allegiance which, in this period, was undeveloped. This is clearly exemplified in the status of the men who were prominent in the early years of the reign. Thomas Osborne, Earl of Danby, (afterwards Duke of Leeds) became Lord President of the Council and, as an experienced bribe-master, succeeded in obtaining narrow majorities for the grants of war subsidies by the Commons. His rival, George Savile, Marquis of Halifax, who might be described as the Elder Statesman, served as Lord Privy Seal, but he lost somewhat in prestige by his conduct of Irish affairs, and retired from active politics in 1690. Two other peers, the Earl of Nottingham and the Duke of Shrewsbury acted, at times, as secretaries of state, in which capacity they wielded some of the powers of a prime minister. But none of these high officers of state had a following in the House of Commons, and they were all thinking of responsibility, not to Parliament, but to the King; moreover, their pre-eminence arose from the older type of office, connected with the Privy Council or the household. Meanwhile, by the middle years of the reign, a new type of minister was emerging from the circumstances created by William's war with France, a war described in the succeeding chapter. This was the head of a department; and, as finance became the supreme consideration, it was natural that the Treasury and Exchequer should provide officials having a less intimate connection with the Sovereign, but a closer

contact with the House of Commons, and even some
responsibility to the nation. This was illustrated most
clearly by Charles Montagu, afterwards Earl of Halifax
who, in the later and critical years of the war, was
Chancellor of the Exchequer and First Commissioner of
the Treasury. To a less extent, Admiral Russell, later
Earl of Orford, who acted as First Commissioner of the
Admiralty, was a representative of this newer type of
departmental minister. These two served under Lord
Chancellor Somers, in the years 1695–98, in an informal
cabinet known as the Junto, probably the only semblance of a ministry in William's reign, because backed
by a Whig majority in the Commons, and responsible
for bringing the country through the last and most
difficult stage of the war.

The members of the Junto were consistent Whigs;
but, after 1698 the Whigs were displaced by Tories
who, led by Robert Harley, maintained their supremacy for the rest of the reign. During these last years
of the reign, William had no minister whom he could
trust; and he had been obliged to sacrifice Somers, the
only prominent Englishman in whom he had any
confidence. So he was obliged to turn for his ministers,
such as they were, to the Tories, and the appointments
of the Earl of Rochester as Lord Lieutenant of Ireland
and of Sidney Godolphin as First Commissioner of the
Treasury showed at least an approach to the principle
of giving high office only to those who could command
a majority in the Commons.

The main exception to this was the King's retention

of Somers as Lord Chancellor until April 1700, in spite of the fact that his party had been in a minority since the autumn of 1698. Another exception was Sunderland, whose personal connection with William in this and the preceding reign has never been fully explained. Sunderland was a very efficient " manager," altogether without scruple, and his efficiency may have been his main recommendation in the eyes of the King, who, in his desire to get things done, was not likely to be deterred by ethical considerations. What seems certain is that the earl at first advised the King to impose his confidence in the Whigs, as the party in favour of the war; and then, after 1698, in the Tories, as the party having a majority in the Commons; it was also known that he favoured the appointment of a small, efficient cabinet, containing representatives of the household, the Privy Council and the departments, from which the King might seek advice. In this way the minister who had had such experience of giving effect to the will of a non-parliamentary sovereign, now applied his knowledge in the service of a parliamentary ruler; and just as the Dutchman William Bentinck, Earl of Portland was the King's chief adviser in foreign affairs, so Sunderland was the informal, even secret adviser in regard to the manipulation of the parliamentary machinery at home. The King was anxious to confer on his confidant some responsible office, and in 1697 appointed him Lord Chamberlain, but such was the dislike of Parliament for James's infamous agent, that he soon had to resign even this household office. Accordingly, in his appointments to high offices of state, and his retention of ministers in these offices, William showed some regard for opinion, mainly as expressed by the House of Commons.

He showed a similar discretion in his use of another element in his prerogative—the veto. He vetoed four public Bills—a Bill to ensure the independence of the judges; the first version of the Triennial Act; a Bill excluding placemen from the Commons; and a Bill imposing high landed qualifications on members of the House of Commons. In the first instance, the King's reason was clear. By the Bill, the salaries of the judges were to be paid from the Civil List; and for this extra burden on his resources the royal consent had not even been asked. The next two were vetoed because they appeared to trench on the prerogative, since the King would otherwise sacrifice his right of determining the life of Parliament, and would be deprived of the support of Placemen in the House; the fourth was banned because it was felt unjust that wealthy townsmen, not possessed of estates, should be ineligible to sit in the Commons. But, in regard to the first Bill, William always respected the independence of the judges, an independence which secured statutory and permanent confirmation by the Act of Settlement. Of the other three, it is notable that, in later years, they all passed into law, but not one proved to be permanent. William's exercise of the veto caused considerable criticism at the time; nevertheless, his use of it can be described as moderate, and implied that, wherever he consented, he was bound. This was something new.

The most important element in William's prerogative was his right to declare peace and make war. His conduct of the war with France aroused some criticism, notably after the defeats of Steenkirk and Neerwinden; but even more resentment arose from the fact that he directed foreign policy mainly by the advice of two Dutchmen, Portland and Heinsius. Here he was technically within his rights, but the magnitude of the war created a feeling that the King should, in matters of such national concern, be guided by native-born councillors, responsible to Parliament. Now, in 1698 and 1700 the King engaged in two successive treaties with Louis XIV and the States General whereby the Spanish Succession was partitioned among the main claimants; but when these treaties became public knowledge, it was feared that they assigned to France too great preponderance in the Mediterranean. Accordingly, in the summer of 1701, the Tory House of Commons impeached the three Whig ministers, Somers, Halifax and Orford who, it was alleged, had been consenting parties to the treaties. These three ministers, no longer in office, had done little more than register the royal will; and, when the House of Lords rejected the impeachments, there was precipitated a constitutional crisis that was ended only by the dissolution of Parliament. Hence, although the impeachments failed, it was made clear that Parliament would no longer tolerate a personal or irresponsible exercise

of this prerogative right; and already, in the Act of
Settlement, there was a clause limiting this right by
the requirement that, without consent of Parliament,
the nation would not be obliged, by a king not a native
of England, to go to war on behalf of territories not in
possession of the Crown. It was a slender restriction,
but at least it was a start. William himself showed
some regard for Parliament by his communication to
both Houses of copies of treaties whereby the nation
was bound; and, if the relations between these two
Houses had been more friendly, it is possible that they
might have combined in the creation of some kind of
committee to advise the King.

Considering the extent of his rights, and the capriciousness with which they had been exercised by some
of his predecessors, the significant thing is how moderate was William's use of his prerogative. He had little
regard for constitutional precedent; by nature, he was
absolutist, sometimes even wilful and obstinate; nevertheless, by some quality of character and intelligence,
he seems to have realised the extent of the confidence
imposed in him, and he set himself to justify that
confidence. Our parliamentary sovereignty dates
from the rule of a king whose powers were scarcely
even defined.

The most interesting development in this reign is
that whereby so many of those who had opposed the
Revolution, or had been lukewarm in the cause of
William, gradually acquiesced in the new order, and
supported the Protestant succession, with its corollary

of parliamentary sovereignty. Before the end of the reign, these men were willing to be known as Tories. It is characteristic of political parties, as of human beings, that, if a concession is made, something is expected in return; and already the Tories, hitherto intent on removing restrictions from a hereditary monarch, were now intent on imposing them on one who derived his title from Parliament. In 1700 the eleven-year-old Duke of Gloucester died; and, as it now seemed certain that neither Anne nor William would have an heir, the succession had to be regulated. There were two sets of claimants, one, by descent from Elizabeth, daughter of James I, who had married the Elector Palatine; the other, the descendants of Henrietta, daughter of Charles I, who had married the Duke of Orleans. The ineligibility of Roman Catholics for the succession excluded all these claimants (estimated to have numbered about 57 persons in 1714) except Sophia, granddaughter of James I (by the Palatine branch), who had married the Elector of Hanover. So, if the Protestant succession was to be preserved, it was obvious that Sophia's son George, born in 1660, was the next heir presumptive, and accordingly it seemed likely that, within a moderate space of time, England would again be ruled by a foreign king. Here was a new problem; the powers used so moderately by a Dutchman, might be abused by a German. An effort to solve this problem was made in the Act of Settlement, passed in the summer of 1701 by a Tory House of Commons. It was to come into force on the death of Anne and William without heirs.

This statute is a good example of give-and-take. On the one hand, the Act limited the succession to Sophia and her heirs; on the other hand, attempts were made to restrict the powers of the future dynasty by applying those restraints which already the Tories had failed to impose on William. It was known that George was a Lutheran; hence a clause obliging the future sovereign to join in communion with the Church of England; another clause required that the King should not leave the kingdom without consent of Parliament; a third that no foreigner should be a member of the Privy Council, or capable of taking lands from the Crown. These last two provisions implied some criticism of William's conduct. Of wider import was the requirement that all high matters of State should be discussed only in the Privy Council, each councillor to give his advice in writing, duly signed—a restriction which would have ruled out altogether the informal Cabinet; equally unworkable, was the exclusion of all office-holders from the Commons, a provision that would have ended the close co-operation between Parliament and the administrative departments which had been one of the most important consequences of William's War. Both of these restrictions were annulled by Parliament even before the Act came into force in 1714.

On the other hand, the Act completed and confirmed the Revolution settlement. The responsibility of ministers was safeguarded by the clause that no royal pardon could be pleaded in bar of an impeachment, though the right to pardon a convicted person still remained with the Crown. The independence of the judges was secured by the enactment that their salaries should be placed on the Civil List, and that they should be removed only by an address of both Houses. At the same time, all the rights and liberties of the subject were confirmed.

These two measures, the Bill of Rights and the Act of Settlement, when taken together, show how, by the mingling of experience with experiment, our Constitution has been made so strong. But there was one other factor accounting for that strength, a factor so implicit and fundamental that it is not even mentioned in any of the statutes. This was the axiom: *The King can do no wrong*, a principle securely established by the provision in the Act of Settlement that no royal pardon could be pleaded in bar of an impeachment. At first sight, the axiom seems no more than an old absolutist or divine-right maxim; actually, it is the reverse. Originally a lawyer's fiction, it had been applied to public affairs by the Whigs, whose starting point was horror of the barbarity and, still more, recognition of the futility, of punishing the King personally for his misdeeds, as exemplified by the tragedy of Charles I. The Whigs found a way out of this difficulty by distinguishing the King from his ministers, and transferring the guilt of the one to the shoulders of the other by means of the lever of impeachment.

So long as the King could grant a pardon in advance, the weapon was useless; but now that the pardon was invalid, Parliament could penalise the minister who had made possible the public misdeeds of his royal master, for the measure of the King's (supposed) innocence, provided the measure of his agent's guilt. As impeachment implied the regular meeting of Parliament, the Whig doctrine was inseparable from parliamentary sovereignty; and, if logically worked out, would deprive the Sovereign of all initiative in matters of State. The fact that public opinion has taken the place of impeachment does not detract from the force of the principle.

For long, the alternative was the Tory doctrine that the King *can* do wrong, that ministers can shield themselves behind the cloak of royal command, and that the subject, oppressed by an iniquitous, but anointed, monarch can do nothing except submit. In 1716, when impeached for his share in the proceedings of the last years of Queen Anne, the Tory Robert Harley, Earl of Oxford attempted to exculpate himself by pleading the command of the Sovereign, a defence which the Whigs described as a " false and malicious libel "; still more, George III, by his exercise of a large measure of public responsibility, showed himself unwilling to recognise the validity of the Whig maxim. Hence a long time elapsed before that doctrine became fundamental in the British constitution. Of that long process, William's reign is the starting point. In the same year as the Tories passed the Act of Settlement, when they impeached the three Whig lords for their alleged part in the partition treaties, they repudiated the excuse of the ministers that they had merely carried out the royal commands. Accordingly, in this oblique way, the Commons tried to transfer responsibility to shoulders other than the King's; whatever his guilt, the King must be kept immune. In effect, therefore, as early as 1701, the Tories were adopting and applying this all-essential Whig maxim against Whigs, and so placing it outside party politics, though they were slow to recognise that the weapon might equally well be used against themselves. From the general, though tardy, acceptance of this principle great consequences followed. Sometimes humanity is influenced more by convenient suppositions than by incontrovertible logic, for it is not always the obvious that determines human action or belief. As the papacy is based on the principle that, in matters of faith, the Pope cannot err, so the British Constitution is founded on the maxim that the King can do no wrong. These two institutions are the most strongly established in the world, possibly because each provides a clear standard of reference, the one for doctrinal error, the other for political wrongdoing.

* 4 *
A King's Failures

THE TITLE of this chapter has reference to William's comparative lack of success in war, and his failure to maintain peace, in spite of almost desperate efforts in both enterprises. That he would have little success as a general after 1689 might have been deduced from the mediocrity of his military leadership after 1672; but his inability to secure peace for Europe arose from no deficiency on his part.

This chapter is devoted to these two aspects of William's kingship. The King had made possible the military conquest of Ireland; his cause had triumphed in Scotland—two episodes which have already been treated as part of the Revolution Settlement in Great Britain. But, as that Revolution was European in its implications, it had to be fought for in a general war against Louis XIV, a war which lasted until 1697, usually designated by historians the War of the League of Augsburg. Unfortunately, in the absence of any strategic planning, there was little co-operation between the English and Dutch allies, nor was there even any co-ordination between their activities on sea and on land, defects which help to account for the ineffectiveness of their campaigns against France. Accordingly, this chapter summarises, first, the contest at sea, and then the contest on land. In the latter, William did little more than offer costly resistance to the progress of French arms. A similar lack of success provides the theme of the later part of this chapter, which describes the King's attempts to avert war by a solution of the Spanish Succession question, attempts which were ended by his death.

Fortified by the support of both Houses of Parliament, William declared war on Louis on the 8th of May 1689. England of the Revolution was unprepared for war. The navy, to the efficiency of which Pepys had devoted both his energy and his genius for administration, was deficient in ships, men and guns; even more serious, there was often reason to suspect disloyalty or inefficiency (or both) among the officers, who might serve William as they had served James. There were too many " gentleman " officers, some of whom, having obtained their commissions by money or influence, were intent on deriving profit, at the expense of their crews, from their numerous opportunities; there was also unjust disparagement, and even victimisation, of the merchant service. In what was left of the army, there existed good material for leadership, as exemplified notably by Marlborough, Talmash and Cutts; but unfortunately, during the greater part of the reign, the first was out of favour, because suspected of Jacobitism, and the others were overshadowed by those foreign generals in whom the King placed his confidence. As a military leader, William showed pertinacity and a strong desire to seek out the enemy, in order to obtain a decisive result; but his health interfered with his campaigning; nor did he possess sufficient mental agility to modify a tactical design when it was seen to be inadvisable. In consequence, he was constantly out-manœuvred.

The lot of the ordinary soldier and sailor was a hard one. Their pay was constantly in arrears; they were ruthlessly exploited by officials, such as slop-sellers and regimental agents; there was insufficient hospital accommodation for their sick and wounded; and, in the field, the wounded soldier was left to be murdered and robbed. So far from being shocked by these things, contemporaries regarded them almost as normal; indeed, the personal sacrifice of the soldier and sailor meant little to a nation which regarded their absence as a good riddance, since otherwise they would be on the gibbet or (much worse) on the rates. But, towards the end of the reign, there was evidence of relaxation of this callous attitude; for charities were established to help distressed seamen and their families, and there were schemes for the education and maintenance of the sons of those who had lost their lives in the war. For the common man, active service was then considered, not as a badge of citizenship, but of its absence; because, in our *ancien régime*, to each class was assigned a definite duty—the freeholder in the country was responsible for the nation's corn and wool; the freeman in the town, together with the merchant, maintained the nation's trade and industry; the professional classes had each a definitely allotted sphere. There remained those who did not fit into any of these categories; it was by them that the nation's battles were fought. In the words of a contemporary, they were " fit to kill and be killed."

The war raised many new administrative problems, in the surmounting of which the army fared better than the navy, because William was on the spot, accompanied by his energetic secretary, William Blathwayt, and so some unity of direction was secured. The army in Flanders was financed by a number of syndicates, helped by the Bank of England, but increasing financial stringency at home very nearly resulted in breakdown; and indeed, the critical thing in the war proved to be finance. This subject is treated in the next chapter, which records progress at home, in contrast with failure abroad. In the continental campaigns, British arms suffered two notable defeats, at Steenkirk (1692) and Neerwinden, or Landen (1693), but defeat is often the prelude to achievement; and it was in the grim ordeal of the battlefield that the great regimental traditions of the British army first took shape. Moreover, William's army included, as well as Englishmen, a large proportion of Highlanders, lowland Scots, Welshmen and Ulstermen, so it was in the comradeship of defeat and disaster that there was first realised that kinship which was afterwards to result in the unity of Great Britain and Northern Ireland.

But this unity contrasted with the heterogeneity of the allied forces over which the King exercised supreme command: In terms of treaties, most of them signed in 1689, there emerged from the League of Augsburg an offensive European alliance, to which Britain and Holland made by far the largest contribution, amounting, at its maximum, to a total of about 200,000 men, or about two-thirds of the whole allied strength. Among the allies were the King of Spain (on behalf of the Spanish Netherlands), the Electors of Bavaria and Brandenburg, the Duke of Savoy, a number of German princes and the Emperor Leopold, each having different reasons for entering the fray, all of them held together only by the tenacity of William. Denmark, though not an ally, supplied troops in return for a subsidy; she also opened her Norwegian harbours to French privateers. Equally ambiguous was the position of the Emperor. He sent about 12,000 men in return for a guarantee that the allies would promote his claim to the whole of the Spanish succession; nevertheless, even with these very favourable terms, he was worried by his association with heretics, such as English and Dutch, and with a usurper, such as William. But for his territorial ambitions, his proper place would have been with Louis XIV. Another Roman Catholic who experienced increasing uneasiness on this score was the Duke of Savoy, who deserted to France in 1696. In other words, William headed a coalition in which religious scruple contended for mastery with territorial greed, and the marvel is that such a motley array held together for so long. It is significant also that, at the conclusion of hostilities, William, suspecting a secret agreement between Leopold and Louis, expressed a fear that the Catholic dynasties were too strong for Protestant Europe; and it is a tribute to the King's statesmanship that what might have degenerated into a religious conflict was maintained as a war against Louis XIV.

The unprecedented size of the British armies put into the field, together with the large navy that had to be provided for, shows that England, hitherto only a naval power, was now confronted, for the first time, with the problems of full-scale hostilities, conducted in Flanders, on the sea, and in the West Indies. Consequently, there had to be speedy improvisation, and this at a time when national effort was constantly prejudiced by the treachery and embezzlement of Jacobite " collaborators." William was probably the worst served of any English king; he scarcely knew whom to trust. As well as this, there emerged a difficulty of a special kind. Except in 1689, the King did not spend a whole year in England, for he was absent in the summer and autumn, at first in Ireland, then in Flanders and finally in Holland. Until her death in 1694, Mary acted for him in England, with the help of an informal cabinet, unknown to the Constitution, and detested by the House of Commons; thereafter, during these royal absences, some of the royal powers

were vested in Lords Justices. This delegation of
responsibility proved of some constitutional importance,
in so far as deputies or *ad hoc* bodies had to administer
national affairs in the King's name; but these bodies,
whose powers were not clearly specified, were obliged
to refer all important matters of policy to the absent
King, who insisted on retaining supreme direction.
This caused serious interference with the conduct of the
war, and was revealed most clearly in naval affairs,
because admirals might have to take their orders,
at different times, from the King, or the Queen, or the
Admiralty, or from a secretary of state, or from a cabinet, or from the Lords Justices. There were occasions
when one of these authorities would omit to send
the necessary directions, assuming that one of the
others would do so, a situation which, at times,
seriously impeded our operations at sea. But, after
all, it takes a long time to build up the executive
machinery necessary for the conduct of a great war,
and in that time there is bound to be muddle and even
disaster.

In two other respects, William's War suddenly
imposed on insular England new problems such as we
associate with European warfare of the twentieth
century. The first of these was an attempt to blockade
the enemy. Acts were passed prohibiting trade with
France, and there was some kind of agreement with
the Dutch in regard to the enforcement of a blockade.
But the two allies had very different views in regard to
this matter, so different that they each went their own

way, the English being intent on a strict blockade, while the Dutch were anxious that the prohibition of enemy trade should interfere as little as possible with their own commerce. Neutrals, such as Sweden and Denmark, aggrieved by interference with their shipping, protested vigorously; and, for a time, maintained some kind of armed neutrality, which severely taxed the diplomacy of William's envoys in the north. Extensive smuggling provided further loopholes in the barrier which the allies tried to erect round the enemy, whose large fleets of privateers succeeded in capturing a great variety of supplies. Moreover, as she was less dependent than either England or Holland on sea-borne trade, France was inconvenienced, but not seriously prejudiced by the blockade, for she still obtained large supplies of smuggled English wool, and exported considerable quantities of claret, usually under some other name. In effect, therefore, this allied blockade was a failure.

The second problem was more serious. Maritime powers have this disadvantage that, in conflicts with other European powers, their shipping will provide obvious targets; this has already been demonstrated in the two European wars of this century. As only merchant ships with their crews and cargoes are involved, the nation may underestimate the seriousness of this menace, since, to an undiscerning public, the fighting fleets do not seem obviously engaged, and the extent of the losses is usually, for the time, concealed. Such proved to be the case in William's War, though

W. F

contemporaries became justifiably alarmed at the high
and steady rate of sinkings, mainly in the Channel and
North Sea. Not till 1708 was the extent of these losses
made public—the figure was of just under 4,000 ships
—a rate of wastage which England could not have long
survived. French concentration on the privateer was
analogous to German concentration on the submarine,
and had to be countered by similar methods, such as
the arrangement of convoys and the provision of
escorts. On the other hand, English privateers
accounted for more than 1,000 enemy ships, so the war
against merchantment had now come to be a serious
factor in European hostilities.

This detachment of warships for Commerce protection diminished the strength of our Navy; uuits of the
Fleet had also to be allocated for maintenance of
communications with Ireland, and for expeditions to
the West Indies; moreover, events, about to be described, interrupted, for short periods, our supremacy
in the Channel and the Mediterranean. Hostilities
at sea began on the 7th of May, 1689 (the day
before the Declaration of War), with the indecisive
skirmish of Bantry Bay, when Admiral Herbert, afterwards Lord Torrington, attempted to break up an
escorted French convoy which had just landed stores
and men. Contemporaries, including the King, suspected that Herbert had shown a lack of dash, as if
he was anxious, not to win a victory, but to preserve
his ships; exactly the same opinion was held in
France regarding the conduct of the French Admiral

Chateau Renault. Soon, the French fleet, under the command of Tourville, could muster a larger number of ships than the combined Anglo-Dutch forces; it was this enemy preponderance that accounted for one of the major defeats in our naval history—that of Beachy Head (30th June, 1690). In this battle, the Dutch, who fought valiantly, suffered considerable losses; but the English admiral, Lord Torrington, managed to retreat eastwards, and eventually brought the greater number of his ships into the Thames. National indignation at this conduct showed how there still lingered the old idea that, at all costs, a decision should be sought, even against an enemy superior in strength; but Torrington, who coined the famous phrase " a fleet in being " was really acting on a newer conception of naval strategy, according to which the primary duty of a naval commander is to preserve his ships, wherever he cannot reasonably hope to win a victory. In this we can trace the beginnings of a more modern conception of warfare. Hitherto, fleets were smaller; merchantmen could quickly be converted for war-like purposes, and there was little to distinguish between navy and mercantile marine. Now, warships, as well as fleets, were larger and more specialised; their crews had to be retained for longer periods; and, though it was still an age of " gentleman " officers, there was at least a recognition of the fact that training is necessary for the evolution of the naval officer. As war came to be more dependent on all the resources of the nation, it was felt that these resources must be carefully conserved, and that a fleet in being is better than a fleet at the bottom.

This was more keenly appreciated by commanders on the spot than by the authorities in Whitehall. Torrington was tried by court-martial, and, though acquitted, he was never again employed at sea. He was succeeded by another " gentleman " commander, Edward Russell, afterwards Earl of Oxford, a cousin of the Whig martyr Lord Russell, who had been executed in 1683. Russell, a man of personal courage and skill, may have derived from the family Whigism certain compunctions and reservations which were to influence his conduct as an admiral; he would serve William, but with a tempered and even critical loyalty. Meanwhile, England was fortunate in this, that France made little of her victory at Beachy Head. Tourville was ordered to destroy a large convoy which had sheltered in Plymouth; but, as he thought this too hazardous, he contented himself with bombarding the seaside village of Teignmouth. Nor did he succeed in destroying English communications with Ireland, where William had won (1st July) the victory of the Boyne, a victory followed by James's precipitate flight back to France. So the events of the summer of 1690 showed on what a delicate balance the Revolution was poised; for victory in Ireland came only one day after defeat at sea. Fortunately for England, Tourville was anxious not to take risks with his fleet, at that time the largest in the history of France.

Nearly two years of active ship-building served to reverse the disparity between the rival navies; moreover, the death of the active French Minister of Marine, Seignelai, was followed by a period of decline in French naval affairs. The result was that, in 1692, the Anglo-Dutch fleets numbered about 80 ships, in contrast with a French total of about 50; accordingly, before leaving for Flanders in the spring of that year, William ordered preparations to be made for a landing on the French coast. For this purpose a large number of flat-bottomed boats were built. On the other side of the Channel, James was also engaged on plans for an invasion, to be conducted from the bay of La Hougue (in the Cotentin peninsula), his troops consisting of French and Irish, with a number of English Jacobites. The landing was to be effected at Torbay. Relying on the increasingly optimistic reports from Jacobite agents in England, James and Louis were convinced that the nation eagerly awaited the return of its exiled king; that the English fleet was inferior in size to the French, and that several of the admirals, including Russell, would come over to the other side. The anxious Queen Mary, who had good reason to suspect the possibility of such treachery, took the wise step of ordering that an assurance of her absolute confidence in the officers and men should be sent to the fleet. Meanwhile, as a precaution, Marlborough was sent to the Tower. So it seemed to the Stuart advisers that the victory, which they had just missed in 1690, would be granted to their cause in 1692. Tourville, sceptical about these reports, was ordered, early in May, to leave Brest with his inadequate force; his eagerly-hoped for victory was to be followed by the invasion from La Hougue.

It was while tacking across the Channel from St. Helens to Cape Barfleur on 19th May that Russell, with the allied grand fleet, fell in with Tourville and his inadequate forces. A fight ensued in which Russell attempted to envelop the enemy ships, but the wind dropped, and by the late afternoon fog descended; otherwise, the battle of Cape Barfleur might have been one of the most decisive in naval history. It proved to be indecisive, in the sense that the French ships, damaged as many of them were, succeeded in getting away, some of them seeking refuge in St. Malo, others in the bay of La Hougue; indeed, except for the extreme disorder of his flight, Tourville's conduct was similar to that of Torrington two years before. But there was a sequel. Rooke, with fireships, entered the bay of La Hougue on two successive days, 23rd–24th May, and burned thirteen of the finest units of the French navy. A substantial part of the enemy force had been destroyed; the others were scattered to the winds, and so the invasion transports were now useless. In England, La Hougue was misspelt La Hogue, and this came to be the name traditionally applied to the battle, for the good reason that the name denoted the site where so much damage had been done, whereas the name Cape Barfleur merely denoted the area where so little had been achieved.

In one more respect events of the summer of 1692 recalled those of two years earlier. Queen and Cabinet were naturally anxious that Russell's victory should be followed by an English landing, preferably at St. Malo, for which purpose troops and transports were assembled at Portsmouth. What the soldiers were to do when they landed on French soil does not appear to have been determined, or even discussed in the Cabinet, though it is possible that William had plans for this expeditionary force. What is certain is that, for more than two months, the Cabinet, represented by Secretary of State Nottingham, maintained a voluminous correspondence with the admiral, at first urging him to pursue the scattered French ships, and then to make arrangements for the landing. But Russell may have thought that, with such an important achievement to his credit, it would be unwise to risk his reputation or his ships in any further enterprise; or he may even have thought that he had already done enough for William's cause. For whatever reason, he persisted in his policy of doing nothing; and, though the transports set sail in August, no landing was effected. For this, he was temporarily relieved of his command.

The battle of La Hogue, like the battle of the Boyne, can be described as decisive, in so far as the first restored our maritime supremacy, as well as thwarting an invasion, while the second saved Ireland from James and Louis. Otherwise, the English record, in this long war, was mainly one of defeat and disaster. The first disaster was the loss of a great part of the large Smyrna convoy in the summer of 1693, when about 400 English and Dutch merchantmen, escorted by Rooke, were attacked by Tourville off Lagos. Many of the ships, with their valuable cargoes, were destroyed, the others were scattered. This loss had some influence on naval strategy, which can be attributed mainly to the initiative of William; for, in the following year he ordered Russell (now restored to command) to take a large fleet to the Mediterranean, where they were to keep station throughout the winter, with their base at Cadiz. But, even in the execution of this design, there was another disaster. The outgoing fleet included a detachment of ships and troops commanded by Berkeley and Talmash, which had been ordered to effect a landing at Camaret Bay, at the southern entrance to the harbour of Brest. That such a landing was intended had been known to the French for months, who had thus ample time in which to erect fortifications; so, when Talmash and his troops landed (8th June, 1694), they were met by heavy fire, and driven off. Talmash died of wounds. Responsibility for this dismal enterprise must be attributed to muddle in the Cabinet, and the almost complete absence of secrecy in our planning.

Such, in brief, were the main incidents in the war at sea. In Canada, an attempt was made to capture Quebec by Sir William Phipps, with a force of little more than 2,000 men, an enterprise so badly planned, that many of the men died, not from wounds, but from privation. In the West Indies, several attempts were made to capture French islands, in which the lead was taken by Sir Christopher Codrington, Governor of the Leeward Islands. These attempts had a chance of success, because the French West Indies were so thinly manned that the English colonists had a clear superiority of numbers. But here again, English enterprise failed from bad planning, or from its complete absence; for the administrative machinery at home could not cope with the new demands suddenly imposed upon it. No regard was paid to climatic conditions in the West Indies; the expeditions were often sent at the wrong time of year, with rations more suitable for the Arctic than for a sub-tropical area. Intense jealousy between the two services, and the incompetence of several " gentleman " officers all combined to render ineffective the attempted conquests of Martinique and Guadeloupe; and the deaths from sickness made the West Indies, like Dundalk and Bombay, the Englishman's grave. But it was not all sheer loss. For the first time, attention was focused on the health of the fighting services, and the high rate of mortality made imperative some kind of reform. Hitherto, the only medical aid provided for soldier and sailor had been that of the surgeon; now it was realised that they may also have need of the physician—one of the discoveries of this war.

In Flanders, though the health conditions were better, conditions prevented William from obtaining the definite decision on which he had set his heart; for, as before, French policy dictated that siege warfare should play the most important role, and that open fighting should be avoided as much as possible. For the first of these, Louis was well served by Vauban, the greatest military engineer of his age; and, for the second, by the Marquis of Luxembourg, a wily old tactician, whose skill in avoiding combat was matched only by his skill when forced to fight. Moreover, the terrain, with its proximity to France, favoured the enemy, since preparations could be made locally in winter for the next summer's campaign. Elaborate earthworks in south-western Flanders provided adequate defence of the French frontier; while French troops on the Moselle made it difficult for the German contingents to join the allies. So far as the French had a plan, it appears to have been to push northwards to Brussels, Louvain and Antwerp, of which the last would have provided a suitable port for the privateers; on his side, William was anxious to invade France, and bring the war to a successful conclusion. But he never achieved this. In Flanders, his movements were impeded by enemy occupation of such great fortresses as Mons and Namur; elsewhere, his fickle ally, the Duke of Savoy, did not respond to William's scheme for an incursion into France through Dauphiné; in the Channel, Russell had failed to effect a landing at St. Malo. So William had to acquiesce in a warfare of marching and counter-marching, in which he might, at any time, be pounced on by Luxembourg.

From the outset of the Flemish campaigns, French

arms were successful, the victory of Fleurus (1690) being followed, in succession, by the capture of Mons and Namur. At Steenkirk, on one of tributaries of the Scheldt, where William was encamped in the summer of 1692, it seemed that at last he had a chance of catching the enemy unawares, for the secretary of the Elector of Bavaria had been caught in the act of spying for the enemy, so the King compelled him to take a dictated letter into the enemy camp, announcing that a large allied foraging party would be out on the next day, 24th July. This was to be the cover for an attack, and it might have succeeded, but the King had chosen his site badly, and Luxemburg quickly rallied his forces from their first confusion. For whatever reason, only a part of the British infantry, led by Mackay, was brought into action, and on this the brunt of the fighting fell. Although Mackay begged his superior officer, Solms, to bring up the main body of infantry— stationed only about a mile away—the Dutch commander refused, and Mackay, with many of his men, was killed. Only by their brilliant covering of the retreat did the Coldstream Guards prevent this defeat from becoming a rout. Later, when petitioned by the House of Lords to entrust the higher commands only to officers of British birth, William refused to dismiss the infamous Solms.

Inferiority of leadership was again revealed in the summer of 1693, when William was badly defeated at the battle known as that of Neerwinden or Landen (19th July). Here, Luxembourg owed his triumph

mainly to superiority in numbers at the time when the
two opposed armies were marching in almost parallel
lines. This appeared to provide final proof that the
King could achieve nothing in open warfare; and
already, his correspondence suggested a doubt whether
the allies would succeed in the objects which they had
set out to accomplish. Only their refusal to admit
defeat held together this Dutchman and his British
troops.

The death of Luxembourg early in 1695 suddenly
altered the character of the war. He had been pre-
ceded by Seignelai and by Louvois, the one active in
naval, the other in military administration; indeed,
much of the French king's success can beat tributed to
these three men. Vauban, it is true, remained; but
he soon lost favour, because he made no secret of the
disgust with which, as a man of intelligence and
humanity, he regarded these futile and costly campaigns. So, in 1695, William, at long last, had his
opportunity. By that time, military strength in
Flanders was immobilised mostly in fortresses and
garrisons; and in the summer, William achieved one
of his few military successes—the recapture of the great
fortress of Namur. This he did, not with the help of
his Dutch generals, but with that of a heroic Englishman, Lord Cutts. But even this could not relieve the
general conditions of stalemate. In numbers, the
opposing forces were now almost equal, but they had
more difficulty in obtaining fodder locally, and even
France experienced a shortage of men and supplies.

Otherwise, the situation was unchanged. On a long view, the French victories were valueless, because not integrated into any general or constructive policy. James was still in uncomfortable exile; William was still seated on an uneasy throne; armies marched and counter-marched, their leaders anxious, above all, to avoid combat; great fleets remained in harbour or at anchor—too valuable to be risked. Even for Louis the glory of war had gone, and only its supreme futility remained. So the French king, the greatest stage-manager in history, resolved that the curtain should be pulled down.

In this failure of the fighting services to secure a decision, there emerged, in the winter of 1695–96, certain factors which seemed likely to produce definite results even more serious for England than military defeat. France, with her greater wealth, was not obliged to devise new methods for raising money, though she had to intensify the harshness of an anti-quated system of taxation, which fell most heavily on the peasants. It was otherwise in England, where the resources of the State had never been exploited in order to provide for large armies, and where, at the time of the Revolution, there were few devices for raising money on credit. Such devices had to be adopted, but their ultimate success appeared very doubtful; because, with each year of the war, there was experienced greater difficulty in raising loans. The bad state of the English coinage led directly to the financial crisis of 1696, by which time it must have appeared to foreign observers that the emergency structure of English public finance—based apparently (as will later be shown) not on capital but on debt—must topple to the ground. Other things encouraged this hope. There was bitter resentment in Scotland at the interference of the English House of Commons with the Scottish proposal for an overseas trading company, afterwards to take shape as the Darien Scheme; and the well-known lenity shown to Jacobite plotters encouraged them to engage in one more attempt to overthrow William and the Revolution. These things were known at Versailles and St. Germains, where it seemed that the time had come for the restoration of James.

News that such a scheme was on foot obliged William, in January 1696, to recall Rooke and the Mediterranean fleet and to station Russell and his ships in the Downs in order to prevent a sortie from Calais or Boulogne, which were filled with transports. The Jacobite plan appears to have consisted of two things —a rising in England, to be headed by Sir John Fenwick, and an invasion from France. The first was ruined by the precipitate action of Sir George Barclay, who contrived a plan to assassinate William as he was passing through Turnham Green; but, as news of the plan leaked out, it was frustrated. Barclay fled; Fenwick went into hiding and was arrested in the summer. Meanwhile James, with a French army, proceeded to Boulogne in March, anxiously waiting for news of the rising in England, ready to return to his throne at the call of his subjects. But there was no news of any such rising; moreover, as it was widely believed that the assassination plot had been encouraged by James, there was a cooling of sentiment in his favour, and so less likelihood of a call for his return. Accordingly, in April the proposed invasion was abandoned; and here ended the attempts of James to recover his throne.

The assassination plot and its failure caused a remarkable revulsion of feeling among Englishmen. Its immediate effect was seen in April, when Parliament passed an Act imposing on office-holders and future Members of Parliament a "loyal association," in terms of which William was declared to be "rightful and lawful king"—the first recognition of the legitimate character of his sovereignty. It is a tribute to the extreme caution of English constitutional procedure that seven years had elapsed since the Revolution before there was a clear enunciation of that legitimacy; and the obligation, under penalty, to recognise this fact made it more difficult for the crypto-Jacobites to continue their depredations. Here indeed, in this year 1696, was the turning point of the reign. But one more difficult corner had to be negotiated, perhaps the most difficult of all. The financial crisis reached its peak in July with the fiasco of the Land Bank, when a proposed loan to the State of two and a half millions resulted in subscriptions of only a small fraction of that amount. Financial collapse, never more imminent in English history than in the summer of 1696, would have led to withdrawal from the war, and the acceptance of humiliating terms. William had just been saved from assassination; England had just managed to escape invasion and bankruptcy, so it was by a very narrow margin that the Revolution settlement was preserved. The gradual recovery from the financial difficulties and the execution of Fenwick in January 1697 were indications that the tide had turned.

These things led directly to the conclusion of some kind of peace. The negotiations were prolonged, but William impatiently cut across them by arranging for personal negotiations between Portland and the French General Boufflers. The treaty was signed at the château of Ryswick, near The Hague, in the autumn of 1697, after prolonged attempts at delay by the Emperor Leopold, who was still intent on using the war as a means of ensuring his acquisition of the whole of the Spanish succession. In terms of the treaty, each participant agreed to restore his conquests, and so things were left very much as they had been in 1689. But Louis recognised William as lawful sovereign of Great Britain, and solemnly undertook not to assist, directly or indirectly, anyone who troubled him in the enjoyment of his sovereignty. As James and his adherents were obviously implied by this stipulation, the treaty, in effect, recognised that the Revolution was an established fact. Louis's violation, within a few years, of this all-important commitment proved to be one of the direct causes of another and greater war—that of the Spanish Succession.

This matter of the Spanish Succession provided Europe's chief diplomatic problem during the last five years of William's reign. Briefly, the situation was that, as Charles II of Spain had no heir, the succession to his kingdom and vast empire was disputed by two sets of claimants, the Austrian and the French, the first having married younger daughters of Philip III and Philip IV, while the second had married elder daughters of the same kings. Both sets of claimants had complicated matters by renunciations, one on condition of a dowry that was never paid, and another, within the imperial Hapsburg family circle, on conditions that were never recognised by the Spanish Court. England had no claim, but she was vitally concerned, because her West India possessions bordered on those of Spain; and, as early as Cromwell's time, she had realised the importance of free access to the Mediterranean. Consequently she dreaded any acquisition of power in these areas by France; still more, she was now one of the most active of the European states engaged in the profitable slave trade. More and more the negro slave was becoming an essential element in her economy, not only because his labour was required in the West Indies, but because, through the Asiento agency, established in Jamaica, England had the monopoly of supplying slaves to the Spanish colonies. The result was that, by the last decade of the seventeenth century, the orientation of European diplomacy

w.   G was more towards the west; and over a dynastic squabble was superimposed those commercial and maritime considerations which were soon to prove of such consequence.

Charles II's persistence in remaining alive had produced steadily increasing tension and indignation within the Hapsburg and Bourbon family circles, until it seemed that their quarrel was incapable of solution. But an event of 1692 appeared, at least to disinterested spectators, to provide a way out. This was the birth of a son, the Electoral Prince Ferdinand Joseph to the Elector of Bavaria by Maria Antonia, the eldest daughter of the Emperor Leopold (by his first wife). The imperial claim was represented by Maria Antonia and her heirs; nor was it invalidated by any renunciation; but the Emperor, anxious to preserve the empire for his elder son Joseph, and the Spanish Succession for his younger son Charles (both by his third wife), caused his daughter to renounce her rights in favour of her half-brother. So the infant prince, who had the strongest of all the claims, was disinherited by a grandfather who appears to have devoted most of his energy to elaborate scheming on behalf of his family. But Spain refused to recognise this renunciation; and, in an age when hereditary right was sacrosanct, it appeared that the Electoral Prince had the best claim. Still more, he had this advantage that, as a Wittlesbach, he was not a member of one of the great European dynasties, and the establishment of his line in the Low Countries, the Mediterranean and the western hemisphere would not obviously prejudice English or Dutch interests. This fact encouraged William to think that a solution could be effected by a partition, in which the lion's share would go to the Bavarian prince. He even thought that England might obtain a few crumbs, such as Ceuta or Oran; but William had to deal with potentates who never gave anything away.

In the few years of peace that followed the Treaty of Ryswick, Louis appeared to become conciliatory, while the Emperor became more intractable. This fact caused William to negotiate with the former, while excluding the latter, and, with the participation of the States General, a partition treaty was signed in October 1698 by the three powers, in terms of which the Electoral Prince was to have Spain, the Indies and the Low Countries; the Dauphin was to have Naples and Sicily, with some Tuscan ports, while the Archduke Charles was to have Milan. The division of the spoils was probably as wise as any that could have been devised in such circumstances; and, though it is true that France was given a preponderance in the Mediterranean, she would have acquired a preponderance wherever she was given territory. For England, the immediate advantage was that a Bourbon would not be established in the Low Countries; otherwise, she obtained no advantage, and so it has to be recognised that William's prolonged efforts to procure a settlement were actuated solely by a desire to preserve European peace. These hopes were soon dashed, for the infant Electoral Prince died in January 1699.

So anxious was William to obtain a peaceable settlement that he negotiated a second partition, and tried,
though without success, to induce the Emperor to join
in the negotiations. The second partition treaty,
entered into by William, Louis and the States General
was signed in March 1700; by its terms, the lion's
share, that is, Spain, the Indies and the Low Countries,
were to be conferred on the Archduke Charles, while
the Dauphin was to have the Italian possessions except
Milan, which was to go to the Duke of Lorraine, in
return for the cession of his Duchy to France. This
treaty was not kept secret.

Within a few months the situation in western Europe
completely changed. In October 1700 Charles of
Spain died, leaving a Will whereby his undivided
possessions were conferred on the Duke of Anjou,
Louis's second grandson. Failing him, the order of
succession was to be the Duke of Berry (Anjou's
younger brother), the Archduke Charles and the Duke
of Savoy. Louis decided to accept the Will, and to
reject the second partition treaty; in doing so, he was
acting in accord with the opinion of Europe, including
that of England and the United Provinces, for it was
held that only by preserving the Spanish empire
intact could peace be maintained. In effect, therefore,
there need have been no war. But Louis, hitherto
almost amicable, now acted in a manner that made
war inevitable. He ruled Spain as if it was his own
kingdom; sent his troops to overrun the Low Coumtries
and to expel the Dutch frontier garrisons; he obtained

from the Paris Parliament a superfluous affirmation of
the right of Philip of Anjou to the French throne if his
elder brother failed to succeed. Contemporaries inter-
preted this to mean that Louis designed to unite the
thrones of France and Spain, and to create some
kind of world empire such as that which Charles V had
achieved. Indeed the year following the death of Charles
produced a situation not unlike that which has been
experienced in the present century, a situation whereby
the potential aggressor, having been secured in the
possession of all that he apparently wanted, so ruthlessly exploited his advantages as to make the continu-
ance of peace impossible.

To William it appeared that all his work would
have to be done over again, and that, for the second
time, he would have to unite English and Dutch against
an enemy now far more powerful than in 1689. But,
in spite of failing health, he applied himself, throughout
the summer of 1701, to the building up of a new
alliance against Louis, an enterprise in which he was
greatly helped by Marlborough, now restored to
favour. For the third time he even tried to effect a
partition, but neither the French King nor the Emperor
would yield an inch. Late in August, with the Emperor
and the States General, he entered into an alliance at
The Hague, of which the professed aims were to procure
" equitable satisfaction " for the imperial claims, and
a guarantee that the crowns of France and Spain
would not be united. As well as these objects, the
allies undertook to ensure that the Spanish Netherlands

would provide a barrier for the Dutch, and that the
French would be excluded from the West Indies.
Here was a medley of aspirations. One set of terms
was designed to ensure freedom in Europe, another to
perpetuate its absence in the plantations of the west, an
inconsistency of which contemporaries were completely
unconscious. In the war that followed Britain did not
succeed in substituting a Hapsburg for a Bourbon on
the throne of Spain, but she established herself in the
Mediterranean; she obtained a footing in Canada,
and extended her possessions in the West Indies;
indeed, it was mainly by means of the great maritime
resources so created that England successfully with-
stood the threats of Bourbon and Napoleonic dictator-
ship.

In the summer of 1701, therefore, the stage was being
set for another war. James II died on 5th September,
1701, and Louis's recognition of his son, the " Old
Pretender " convinced the majority of Englishmen
that there could be no peace with Versailles. Already,
in spite of party faction, public opinion was showing
increasing support of William's policy. This was
because a new and vigorous journalism, together with
the public conduct of Louis XIV, had imparted to the
people some measure of political education, and so the
nation which went to war with France in 1702 was
very different from the nation which had been brought
into the war against Louis in 1689.

The last year of William's life must have been a
melancholy one. As well as ill health, he experienced

the animosity of the House of Commons against his former ministers, notably Somers, the only English statesman for whom he showed any personal regard; and he may well have resented the implied criticism, in the Act of Settlement, of his foreign advisers and of his long absences from England. For the third time, he had failed to bring peace to Europe by negotiation and compromise; he had spent himself and the resources of two nations in an apparently futile struggle against the menace of Versailles. It seemed that his failures in war were matched only by his failures in peace. But it was in this last year that there appeared, for the first time, a certain community of feeling between King and Nation, as if the one had imparted to the other something of that high sense of seriousness and responsibility by which his life was directed. He died on 8th March, 1702, but not before he had expressed what was to be his last wish—that there should be a legislative union between England and Scotland. Into his life of 52 years he had compressed years of intense, purposeful effort, of which he was not destined to see the fruits. Superficially, it appeared that he was a failure. But he had restored a nation; he had confirmed its essential Protestantism, and he had put it on the course leading directly to the maritime supremacy of the world. He had come to an England at the mercy of her King; he left an England well able to look after herself.

* 5 *

A Nation's Achievements

THE LIFE of a king is sometimes, in microcosm, the history of a reign, for there may be such a degree of interconnection between ruler and subject that it is difficult to disentangle the two, and so the biography of a monarch may be little more than a record of public events. This is particularly true of William, because his initiative was so great, and because his personality, though never a popular one, gradually exerted an unexpected and unusual influence. The present chapter is concerned with those developments of English civilisation which, directly or indirectly, can be associated with the rule of William III.

Among the many things which we would condemn in William's England were the barbarity of the criminal law and the attitude to the poor. Of the first it may be said that the surest criterion applicable to a young civilisation is this: how far does it protect private property? In the past, human life had none of the sanctity which it possesses to-day, so it had to defend itself; more pressing seemed the need to look after property, which cannot protect itself. This is why so many of the old felonies arose from those misdemeanours that jeopardised a man's possessions; only after these were secured could the legislator turn to the protection of the person. This process was slow; meanwhile, in 1702, when sentencing a woman to death for an offence against property, a judge of King's Bench boasted that nowhere else in the world was property so well protected as in England. What to us seems barbarity, appeared, at the time, evidence of a high degree of civilisation. Then, as regards the attitude to the poor. This word was applied not only to paupers, but to all who had no accredited place in the small, exclusive state. Hence, it included soldiers, sailors, casual labourers, cottagers and the unemployed, all of them only on the fringe of society, dependent on wages or charity, and entitled to no more than the barest means of subsistence. Their work, it was held, merely kept them off the rates. But this rate-shy England, by means of minimum wages at home and negro slavery abroad, created that wealth whereon so much of our modern prosperity is based. In all these respects William's reign was no more than part of a long period in which such injustices passed without comment, except by a few who were considered " cranks." William's reign brought into prominence one of the greatest " cranks " of all time— Daniel Defoe.

The population of England was then about five and a half millions, of whom nearly one-half were the

" poor " as thus defined. Their low wages were an essential element in English economy, for the product of their labour provided the staple articles of export on which our overseas commerce was based. Of these exports, the most important was cloth, made from the native wool which, because of its abundance, quality and variety, appeared to confer an advantage amounting almost to a national monopoly. Influenced to some extent by the example of the Dutch, our statesmen insisted on a policy intended to make England the centre of a great import and export trade, in which our ships would always be provided with profitable freights, while our seamen would have the training in seamanship so necessary in naval warfare. Almost every other consideration was sacrificed to these objects. From stations on the west coast of Africa we obtained gold and ivory as well as negroes; from India we were importing muslins, calicoes, saltpetre and a great variety of fancy goods; from the Levant and Persia came large consignments of silk; from Virginia and Maryland, tobacco; from the West Indies, sugar. For all these commodities there was a demand not only at home, but in Europe, notably in the Mediterranean countries; the Spanish colonies could, in spite of official restrictions, take almost all that we could send. Accordingly, national prosperity in this period was based on overseas trade, wherein our cloth provided the main export, in return for which we imported from two hemispheres a vast quantity of goods, mainly for re-export. The essential things in this economy were cheap labour, abundant shipping and free access to the oceans and harbours of the world.

It was in William's reign that Englishmen became acutely conscious of this maritime basis of prosperity and of the threats of other European powers to that prosperity. A series of Navigation Acts had tried to direct the colonists to the production of the commodities in demand for the re-export trade, and these Acts also strove to ensure that the mother country would, as far as possible, keep the Empire to herself. But the straining of these resources in war prompted statesmen to think of a measure less repressive and more constructive; a measure which, by exploration of circumstances at home and potentialities abroad, would better enable us to co-ordinate these twin elements in the old system. This was achieved in 1696 by the institution of the Council of Trade and Plantations which, as its name implies, was intended to link more closely the opportunities of the Empire with fuller exploitation of our labour resources, in order to expand our markets, and increase national wealth and power. This Council proved to be the ancestor of both the Board of Trade and the Colonial Office. Its establishment was an illustration of a comparatively new principle in administration, namely, that before there can be effective regulation, there must be inquiry into and knowledge about what is to be regulated.

Meanwhile there had been a steady increase of national wealth; and, by 1688, it was noted that the fiscal system did not adequately tap this increased

wealth. Nor were investment facilities adequate for
the large accumulation of savings, in spite of the
existence of joint-stock enterprises such as the East
India Company. Now William's War imposed unprecedented demands for large sums on a nation which
hitherto had thought of wars as short and cheap, so
here was a chance of fructifying accumulated capital,
the interest on which would be paid from the proceeds
of the taxes. Of the taxes, the most important were
the Land Tax, the Customs and the Excise. The Land
Tax, which fell mainly on rents, became permanent,
and by Anne's reign yielded about two millions per
annum, or the equivalent of 4s. in the £; in William's
reign its total yield was about nineteen millions.
Customs and Excise each accounted for about thirteen
millions, and the total amount raised from the taxes
in William's reign appears to have amounted to about
sixty millions, of which at least forty millions were
devoted to the cost of the war. In theory therefore
it might have been possible to pay a large part of that
cost from current revenues, but for two facts, namely,
that the civil administration at home had to be provided for, and that, as ready money was needed at
once, there had to be extensive borrowing at high
rates of interest. For the purpose of loans, Excise
proved the most useful security, because its rate could
be increased without causing great hardship (this was
an age of cheap food and drink); it could be extended
to other commodities, such as salt, and it was not
saddled with any traditional commitment. It was

by far the most important of the indirect taxes, everyone, rich and poor, contributing a share, hence its
resilience and dependability, the two qualities providing the best bases for the floating of large loans.
But for the Excise, it is doubtful if England could
have financed her first great European war.

As the proceeds of the first year of a tax were not
usually harvested until about eighteen months after its
grant by Parliament, and as hostilities demanded the
raising of large sums at once, resort was made to a
device, not entirely new, but now applied regularly
and consistently. This was to embody in each Money
Bill a clause inviting a loan of specified amount, at a
specified rate of interest, on the security of the revenue
to be raised from the tax authorised in the Bill. Behind
this legislative apparatus some unexpected things
were concealed. Thus, the student will search in vain
for any statute which obviously and directly establishes
the Bank of England, but he will find a " Tonnage
Bill " (1694), imposing extra Excise duties on beer
and ale, as well as new duties on imported cargoes,
from the proceeds of which interest was to be paid, at
just over eight per cent, to those persons who, having
contributed to a loan of over a million, might be incorporated as a bank. The loan, with security for payment of its interest, came before the bank, because it
was so much more urgent. So too with what we call
the National Debt. This cannot be fathered on any
statute, for practically all the Money Bills of this reign
invited a public loan, which was repaid only in part,

hence an accumulation of separate debts of greatly
varying amounts.

Each of these loans was tied to the fund specified in
the Act—this was a virtue in so far as an arbitrary
transfer of security could not be effected—but it was
also a defect, because, on failure or deficiency of the
fund, all the payments based thereon would be prejudiced. The revenues from the various taxes were
thus kept quite distinct, like the cells of a honeycomb,
and the Exchequer tally, with its written order for
repayment, specified the fund from which alone payment could be made. In other words, the nations of
western Europe still did their accounting as many
children do, that is, each item of receipt and expendi-
ture was kept apart, and there was no thought of
consolidation; nor was there any question of supple-
menting a deficiency in one source from a surplus in
another. Hitherto, therefore, lending money to the
State had been both technical and risky, so it is not
surprising that, before 1689, most of the lenders were
goldsmiths and bankers, who might be expected to
have some knowledge of the solvency of the source on
which their loan was placed. But even these experts
had suffered from the Stop of the Exchequer in 1672,
so there was needed some ingenuity to induce the
public to lend large sums for long periods. This
difficulty was overcome, and after the Revolution,
public finance ceased to be a private gamble.

The lead in devising measures for this purpose was
taken by a newcomer into politics, Charles Montagu,

later Earl of Halifax, who became Chancellor of the
Exchequer in 1694 and First Commissioner of the
Treasury in 1697. He adopted what, for the time,
was probably the right policy—he combined security
(so far as that was attainable) with an appeal to the
gambling instincts of his contemporaries. In the
schemes which he devised, one could be sure of one's
money, in the sense that interest would be regularly
paid; but one might also hope to gain something in
the more speculative enterprises that were launched,
particularly in the lotteries. The first of these, security,
was ensured by an Act of 1697 which allocated fresh
revenues for the specific purpose of making good
deficient funds, a measure which, for the first time,
ensured a certain consolidation, so that thenceforth
the lender had the backing of all the national revenues
for his loan. It was in this way that what we call the
National Debt came to be established though, for long,
it was not considered permanent, since it was no more
than a series of deficiencies on the funds which, as
they derived from a period of emergency, would be
redeemed by a period of normality. That so many
people lent money on these funds is proof of national
confidence, and that this confidence should be held
inviolate was the injunction of one of William's last
speeches to Parliament. The return of the Stuarts
would have meant the repudiation of these obligations.
Hence a large and influential section of the nation had
a vested interest in William's retention of the throne.

The other, the speculative element, was of less importance, but one of the gambles had some indirect social consequences. In 1692 Montagu induced the Commons to pass an Act inviting a loan of a million guaranteed by an additional Excise, granted for 99 years—our first long-term loan. The lenders were given two options. For each unit of £100 subscribed, they might elect for a straightforward life annuity of fourteen per cent; or they might join in a tontine, whereby they would receive a life annuity from a fund which was augmented as annuitants died off, so that, by speculating on the length of one's life or that of a nominee one could hope to provide a good income in old age. Readers of *The Wrong Box* by R. L. Stevenson and Lloyd Osborne will not need to be reminded of the family complications to which a tontine might give rise, since expectant relatives were anxious that their venerable ancestor should live long enough to win the last lap of the longevity stakes. But Montagu's scheme, as it applied to an annuity, and not to a capital sum, attracted only a minority of " adventurers," the majority preferring the more humdrum fourteen-per-cent annuities. As the sum raised by this experiment was short of a million, the Chancellor of the Exchequer invited subscriptions for the amount of the deficiency, and, at the same time, enabled subscribers, on payment of an extra sum, to convert their life interests into annuities for the unexpired part of ninety-nine years. In this way, the tontine and life rent gave way to the long-term investment, by means of which one could provide, not only for oneself, but for dependents and survivors. Here was a revolutionary change because, hitherto, this " cover " had been available only for the owners of land. Moreover, these annuities were tax-free, a concession which caused a number of landowners, burdened by the heavy Land Tax, to place their money in these popular government stocks. Although Montagu had not been able to make much use of the tontine, nevertheless, that old gamble contained a principle—that of survivorship—which led directly to life assurance; indeed, the earliest schemes for that purpose (organised by private persons) were tontines of husband and wife.

Most important of these financial achievements were the foundation of the Bank of England and the reform of the silver coinage. In 1694 Montagu revived, in a modified form, a scheme originally proposed by William Paterson, when he invited subscriptions to a loan of £1,200,000, the interest on which was to be paid from a guaranteed annual sum of £100,000 which, in its turn, was to be raised from new tonnage and Excise duties. Provided the capital was subscribed, the lenders were to be incorporated as a bank, with authority to issue a paper currency. The success of the scheme was very striking, for, by the summer, the greater part of the loan was subscribed and handed over to the State in return for an equivalent amount of tallies, mostly at a discount. The subscribers were mainly the great Whig financiers of London. But few institutions have had such a precarious infancy as the Bank of England. Montagu had great difficulty in raising even the promised annual sum of £100,000; and, for a time, the new institution was dependent for solvency on the integrity of its directors and the forbearance of its creditors. In 1697 the Bank again came to the help of the State with a further loan of about a million; and so, in a financial crisis, the Bank of England proved a stabilising factor. Here, for the first time in our history was a demonstration of the power of that mighty, but intangible thing which we now call " the City."

But the greatest difficulty of all had yet to be surmounted—the coinage. The undervaluing of silver at the Mint had, for some time, caused a steady export of scrap silver, mainly to Holland and the east, the scrap consisting of clippings from the unmilled, irregularly-shaped coins. Clipping became a hobby or even a minor industry; with some, it was even considered " patriotic," with the result that, by 1695, serious dislocation was caused at home and abroad by the greatly depreciated state of this, one of the elements of a bimetallic currency. With the help of Newton and Locke, Montagu devised an entirely new silver coinage, made from old coins and plate, the cost of which was borne by a new and unpopular tax, the Window Tax. It was a long time before the new coins, with their milled edges, found their way into circulation, but meanwhile the currency was supplemented by paper money, such as Bank of England notes, and the Exchequer Bills which Montagu introduced in 1696. This led to a change of great social and economic importance. At that time, it was treason to counterfeit the coin of the realm, and death was the penalty; but, for a first offence, forgery was no more than a misdemeanour, and the pillory was the penalty. With so much paper money in circulation, there was a serious danger of loss by forgery, so, by statutes of 1696–97, it was enacted that the forgery of Exchequer Bills or Bank of England notes was a felony, punishable by death. A few years later, it was ruled by Lord Chief Justice Holt that a person losing bank notes or securities would have an action at law against the person into whose possession they had come, because these valuables, unlike coin, are distinguishable by their markings. In these ways, therefore, England obtained a more dependable currency, since the silver coins were now of full weight, and paper money was accorded some protection against both the forger and the thief. Only thus, indeed, could England have become a great trading state.

In one more respect there was provided at least a stimulus for an advance in public integrity. It was still almost fashionable to evade payment of one's debts, for, in this intensely religious age, the satisfying of one's creditors was regarded (except by the Quakers) not as a moral obligation, but as a social convention, a fact to which the well-filled debtors' prisons bore eloquent testimony. This convention was encouraged by the example of Members of Parliament who, in consequence of their parliamentary privilege, could delay payment for so long that the debt might be wiped out altogether by pleading a statute of limitations, which restricted the period within which an action could be brought. In 1701 a Tory House of Commons set a much needed example by passing an Act which limited parliamentary privilege to such an extent that most of our law-givers were thenceforth obliged to pay their debts.

This instance may be cited as an example of how a political party might introduce a reform having little obvious connection with the principles traditionally attributed to that party. In the past, historians applied the terms Whig and Tory much too freely to the politicians of this period, on the unquestioned assumption that there was then a clear-cut distinction between them, recognised in the Commons, and extending to the constituencies. But, throughout the greater part of William's reign, there were still many who refused to accept these labels (they were still nicknames); and there were even some who deplored anything like a dualism in the House; still more, the voters, where they were not influenced by bribes, were thinking of family connection rather than party principles. This can be illustrated from one fact alone, to which little attention has hitherto been paid. All the English counties and practically all the English boroughs each returned two members; accordingly, had there been any party allegiance, each pair would usually have been in agreement in regard to any important issue. The facts show that this was not so, even in those cases where the two members are supposed, on modern classifications, to have been of the same party. Here is a characteristic of parliamentary life as it was developing in William's reign. Many members came to Westminster uncommitted to any party, but often associated with some group; sooner or later an important question would arise in the House—it might be that of offering the Crown to William, or voting grants for the war, or signing the Loyal Association, or disbanding the army—and on each occasion there would be a hot contest between two sharply opposed sides. It was this almost invariable dualism, precipitated by some important question or event, that distinguished the old House of Commons; and in such a dualism it followed that a single topic would be debated from a number of different angles. The system was not unlike that of a modern brains' trust, where each question is handled on its merits, whereas in the present-day parliamentary system, each question may have to be decided in terms of party management. This alone helps to account for the vigour of the old unreformed House of Commons, and for the fact that while our legislation often reflects the interests of a class, it seldom reflects the convictions of a party. The Bill of Rights had provided that there should be no interference with freedom of debates or of proceedings in Parliament, and it was in this freedom that influential Englishmen acquired their unrivalled knowledge of the many problems arising from life in the State.

As the freeholders governed England, it was natural that the interests of the landed classes should have first place in the preference of the legislators. But already, in William's reign, there had begun a movement which was destined ultimately, not to break down class distinction, but to create a more sympathetic understanding between classes. There were two Englands, an upper and a submerged half; the one respectable, the other disreputable. Charles II's Court had popularised licentiousness and libertinism among the upper classes, but the same qualities, when manifested by the poor, were named profaneness and debauchery, vices heavily penalised by an overburdened moral code. Now, after the Revolution, there was a reaction against many things characteristic of the preceding régime. It was the opinion of most responsible Englishmen, including staunch Loyalists and Anglicans, that a considerable part of the nation had been corrupted by the example of the later Stuarts, and that reform must begin with the enforcement on the humblest classes of those moral edicts, the promulgation of which had provided the one point of agreement between Crown, Lords and Commons. Accordingly, small bodies of churchmen began to be formed about the year 1692, who patrolled the streets on Sundays in order to report those tradesmen and others who carried on their occupations on that day; while, with the help of informers, they obtained convictions for more serious offences, such as keeping disorderly houses. A compendium of the moral legislation was circulated among these volunteers, who also met at regular intervals, when they avoided points of dogmatic theology and prayed for the state of the nation. At first sight, it appeared that few movements could be more narrow than this. But, within a few years, it was joined by the Dissenters; it spread to Scotland, Ireland and the Plantations; and, before the end of the reign, it was regarded as a great campaign for the moral reform of the nation. It had the support of the King and the bishops; and so the tale-bearers, who had set out merely to enforce class legislation on the poor, found themselves in the vanguard of a great movement intended to promote a higher standard of life and conduct among all classes. The debauchery of the rich now seemed almost as reprehensible as the " debauchery " of the poor.

It was in this way that the two Englands succeeded in acquiring some knowledge of each other. With the knowledge thus acquired of conditions among the humble, these reformers came to adopt a more humane attitude by their realisation that destitution and even crime are not always the consequences of bad morals, but, as often, of bad social or economic conditions; indeed, these amateur policemen may be regarded as among the remote ancestors of the modern charity worker. Stages in that process are marked by the institution of schemes to collect money for necessitous widows, or for the distressed families of sailors; and in 1701 the House of Commons proposed to investigate the whole question of charitable trusts, in order that their funds should be applied to their proper objects. The Society for the Promotion of Christian Knowledge was formed in 1696, a branch of which, the Society for the Propagation of the Gospel, extended its activities even to the negroes in the plantations. Hence, before the end of the reign, many of the characteristic qualities of the later Wesleyan movement had been anticipated, and already England was endowed with that strong spirit of Evangelicism which was to prove of such social consequence.

Hitherto, initiative, in these matters, had come from the State, and that initiative had usually been repressive. Now, much had been done by the efforts of volunteers. This, in itself, was important, if only because it showed how much can be effected by the sustained efforts of minorities, working for a definite cause. It may even be hazarded that, in consequence of the success of this movement, Governments thenceforth acquired some measure of sensitiveness to what is called public opinion, a public opinion created by pioneers, and spread by a rapidly expanding journalism and a comparatively free Press. The influence of the movement can also be seen in literature, for the obscenity of the two previous reigns went out of fashion, and there was even a demand for the abolition of stage plays. But the stage just managed to survive; moreover, with the ending of the Press Censorship in 1695, there was a great broadening out of literature, because the author had now to consider, not the censor, but the reading public, whose taste, as it was more indeterminate, or even more fickle, called for greater powers of adaptation on the part of the writer. In this way, journalism came into its own, and a new type of composition came into vogue—novels and dramas based on "sensibility," a word which meant, not common sense, but sensitiveness. The "sensible" person, distinguished by an extreme delicacy of feeling was being evolved, destined soon to satiate eighteenth-century readers with orgies of sepulchral gloom and celestial exaltation, and, later, to prepare the way for the Romantic Revival. Nor was this a mere literary convention, for it was eloquent of that richer humanity which can be detected, however faintly, in the national life of William's reign.

Some evidence for this claim can be adduced from an unexpected quarter—the Statute Book. This was not a humanitarian age; hence the importance of even the most tentative beginnings of a new conception of human life. Such a beginning can be found in the Bill of Rights, which contained a clause condemning "cruel and illegal punishments," possibly the first provision of its kind in English history. There is no doubt that the legislators had Jeffreys in mind; here, indeed, was a breaking of that "silence" by which the judge's apologists set such store. Reaction against the immediate past can be seen also in the Trial of Treasons Act, which, because of prolonged disputes between the two Houses did not become law until 1696, a reform which ended some of the worst abuses in trials for treason by enacting that the accused should be allowed to retain counsel, and that he should be supplied with a copy of the indictment ten days before trial. It this way it became more difficult for the Crown to obtain a conviction in political cases—hitherto it had been held that, for this purpose, the crown should be impeded as little as possible by legal formalities—and Jeffreys, with his colleagues, had shown how easily these formalities could be dispensed with. Thenceforward the Crown conformed more closely to normal procedure, not because it was more secure, but because it was more humane. Here also is the answer to those who maintain that, in the seventeenth century, the safety of the state was dependent on the infliction of cruel punishments, for in William's reign, when the Throne was so insecure, it was found possible to eliminate some of that brutality which had appeared necessary in order to keep a legitimate crown on the heads of the Stuarts. In other words, the Tower and the block were ceasing to be the sole answer to critics of the Government. A similar quality of mercy can be seen in an Act of 1698 whereby a convicted atheist was to suffer, for a first offence, no more serious penalty than loss of his office. Elsewhere, the penalty was death. Accordingly, in the England of William's reign, both Christianity and Sovereignty ceased to be dependent, for their validity, on the hangman.

These things provide evidence of a change of mentality, however slight, in the decade after the Revolution. Can William's reign be associated with anything distinctive in the intellectual or imaginative achievement of the nation? It is usually hazardous to connect such achievement with a reign, particularly one of such moderate length as that of William; even more, because that reign came towards the end of a period of supreme intellectual achievement, dominated by Newton, whose *Principia* was published in 1687, a period distinguished by Purcell, who died in 1695, by Wren, who was now being displaced by younger men, and by Dryden, who had outlived his greatest achievements long before his death in 1700. But there was one incident in William's reign which was destined to have great influence in the development of English life and civilisation. This was the termination of the Press Censorship in 1695. Thereafter, freedom of the Press was limited only by the law of libel which, at that time, extended to all expressions of opinion about the conduct of the State. Otherwise the author was free. The first book to illustrate this new freedom was John Toland's *Christianity Not Mysterious*, published in 1696, a book which popularised Deism, a system acceptable to those who were no longer able to believe in a literal creed. Hence the development of systems of Natural Religion, such as were afterwards brought into vogue by Shaftesbury. None of these movements was directed against the clergy, nor against the Church of England, which, indeed, became more securely established in the later years of the seventeenth century; accordingly that Church, having made its truce with scepticism and dissent, survived to enjoy its long slumber of the eighteenth century, disturbed only by the emergence of the Wesleyan and Evangelical movements. So Christianity in England gained in breadth what it lost in monopoly.

This broadening of national life and wider diffusion

of intellectual activity can be connected with the
stimulus provided by William's War, for both these
characteristics were clearly evidenced in the years after
the conclusion of peace. Generalisation is impossible,
but one assertion may be made of this more ample and
diversified England, that it was not an age of poetry.
Dryden, the last of the great seventeenth-century poets,
was succeeded as poet laureate by Thomas Shadwell
and Nahum Tate, of whom the latter plumbed depths
seldom exceeded even in the annals of the laureateship.
So far as the King was concerned, that did not matter,
because he was no reader, least of all of poetry, and
his subjects were now content with verse which, in its
aptness, became little more than a supplement to
polite conversation. Thereafter, poetic inspiration was
as carefully clipped and trimmed as the hedges at
Hampton Court. But there was some compensation.
Using French models, Dryden had brought almost to
perfection a comparatively new mode of expression—
the essay. Now, the distinctive thing about the essay
is that, in a sequence of paragraphs, a theme is eluci-
dated from different angles in such a way that many-
sided opinion takes the place of direct assertion.
Moreover, what might formerly have been a flat slab
of prose, is now so carefully divided into paragraphs
that the plain surface becomes a series of contours, by
means of which the reader can follow, in its numerous
gradations, the train of thought passing through the
author's mind. Just as the folio was succeeded by the
more easily-handed octavo and duodecimo, so the

interminable perorations of the erudite were followed
by a succession of well-arranged paragraphs in which
the author could maintain the interest of his reader.
But the significance of this medium of expression was
more than literary. The essay lends itself readily to
the expression of opinion, or rather to comparison of
different opinions; it demonstrates how there are
usually at least two sides to every question. By its
vogue, especially as popularised by the new journalism
after 1697, the essay helped to discredit the old dog-
matism, and to prepare the way for a more rational
and tolerant England.

The diffusion of intellectual activity in this age has
been somewhat obscured by the pre-eminence of
Newton. That pre-eminence was the pinnacle of a
structure which had a very wide base, for the subjects
now classified as the sciences were, at that time, neither
closely specialised nor clearly differentiated; on the
contrary, they all invited free entry by every man of
inquiring mind. Hence the antiquaries and topo-
graphers—all of them engaged in the discovery of
England—included botany and geology in their
province, if for no other reason than that their field
work brought them into contact with plants and fossils.
Subjects were not partitioned off as they are to-day.
Newton himself dabbled in theology: Wren was of
great eminence as mathematician and astronomer;
Hans Sloane, as a young doctor in the West Indies,
collected plants and made records of climate. Robert
Plot, the first public teacher of chemistry in Oxford,

was not a professor of that subject, but the keeper of a great collection of antiquities bequeathed to the University by another antiquary, Elias Ashmole. Of this intellectual diversity, good examples are provided by the physicians, some of whom, originally in holy orders, had been obliged to leave the church because of their latitudinarian opinions. An example of this forced migration to a secular pursuit was Richard Morton who, in the early years of William's reign, published the results of his clinical observations of tuberculosis, the starting point of scientific study of this subject.

There were other respects in which this intellectual curiosity was to prove of practical consequence. The strong mathematical element in English education had already impelled such men as Petty and Graunt to the study of population and life statistics; indeed, society, in England as elsewhere in western Europe, was becoming much more self-conscious, in the sense that it was now interested in such entirely fresh topics as the number of human beings in each unit of civilisation, and their average expectation of life. The Hearth Tax returns provided a rough estimate of the number of households in England and Wales; it was on this basis that Gregory King compiled the first serious estimate of our population and of its constituent elements. Characteristically, King was not by profession a statistician, but an engraver, antiquary and herald who devoted ingenuity and industry to study of the human and economic bases of English society. Similar interests inspire the work of Charles Davenant, son of the dramatist, who, in 1705 was appointed Inspector-general of imports and exports. His numerous writings were concerned mainly with our overseas trade and their repercussions on industry at home; indeed, it may be claimed of him that he was the first Englishman to apply statistical methods to economic problems. These investigations were encouraged also by the inquiries and reports of the committee of Trade and Plantations which had been set up in 1696, as also by the activities of the Royal Society. All this provides some evidence of the more dynamic and purposeful England which emerged from the Revolution of 1688.

In conclusion, it may be asked whether any Englishmen, notable in spheres other than politics or war, can be closely linked with the reign of William, or, even if indirectly, with the King himself. There were three men for whom such a claim can be made. These were Daniel Defoe (1661–1731), John Locke (1632–1704) and Sir John Holt (1642–1710). In very different ways all three contributed to the evolution of an England whose rapid progress, moral as well as material, belied the convictions of those who had thought that the Revolution was no more than a restoration.

Holt, who was profoundly learned in the old common law, became Lord Chief Justice of King's Bench in 1689, and he had this amount of connection with the King that he was never interfered with, an important point, for it meant that he was the first judge for at least a century who could pronounce his judgments

without fear of the displeasure of the Crown. Many of
his decisions have passed into our case law, and of
these several have helped to enlarge the freedom of
the individual, notably in his decisions regarding the
rights of the subject against privileged bodies. A
lawyer of singular acuity of intellect, he was also a man
of humanity, so far as that virtue was possible in a
judge of that time. This was shown in his handling of
cases which came to him on appeal from the Poor Law
authorities, cases where the children and dependents
of the poorest were concerned; the same quality was
manifest in the procedure of his court, for he insisted
on a standard of evidence higher than that which had
usually prevailed, sometimes acting almost as counsel
for the accused when the testimony of hostile witnesses
had to be probed. It was this quality which caused
him to discredit prosecutions for witchcraft; indeed,
he was the first English judge to declare that the prose-
cutors in these cases were impostors. Generally,
therefore, it may be claimed that the judicial bench
was redeemed by Holt from the infamy of the preceding
régime. At least one of his decisions was remarkable.
As the negro was a chattel, he might, even when in
England, be sued for as an article of merchandise, and
recovered by an owner who had lost him. This was
the practice until early in William's reign. But in that
reign, there was formulated an entirely new principle,
for in the case of *Smith v. Browne and Others*, an action of
debt, the owner of a slave lost his case, and in the
course of the proceedings Holt declared that as soon

as a negro comes to England he is free. This was a momentous pronouncement, because it marked the beginning of a complete change in the attitude to human life.

Locke had this connection with William that he came to be regarded, at home and abroad, as the almost official exponent both of the principles of the Revolution and of the type of kingship that followed. By profession a physician, he had been deprived of his studentship at Christ Church, Oxford, in the year 1684; a philosopher, he wrote on subjects having a wide social import—on the principles of human understanding, on toleration, on education, and on statecraft. Rejecting the old doctrine of innate ideas, he based understanding, not on the intuitive, but on the perceptive, and so linked it with the senses. To the education of the young he made a new approach, in so far as he considered the child, not as inferior to his elders, but as superior in at least this respect that, though uninformed, he is still intellectually honest, and so his questions should be treated seriously. There was a similar novelty in his conception of toleration, which he regarded as a social virtue, manifested only by those who are essentially social, and to be denied only to those who are incurably anti-social. This social element was a quality of character generated by experience of life in the State. To this, at least an approach had been made in the Toleration Act of 1689, which made concessions to those who, though outside the Established Church, had proved themselves loyal citizens, while denying any concessions to those who, whether from their principles or associations, were still suspected of disloyalty. In this way, toleration was secularised; and though the Roman Catholics were still (unjustly) excluded, nevertheless they enjoyed a measure of freedom greater than that accorded to many religious minorities on the Continent.

This secular element can be seen also in Locke's treatises on government. He began by rejecting the divine right conception of sovereignty, a conception based on pedigree, and confirmed by anointing with the holy oil. In place of divine decree and sacerdotal sanction, Locke substituted the social contract, whereby the prerogative of the ruler was harmonised with the rights and duties of the subject. Locke's ideal monarch is essentially an English gentleman, exercising his powers with circumspection and restraint, his natural sagacity and responsibility to his fellow-men taking the place of the old divine intention and responsibility to God alone. As well as this, Locke popularised a convenient formula. In his analysis of the English Constitution as it had evolved from the Revolution, he divided it into the three constituent elements, executive, legislature and judiciary, each supreme and independent in its own sphere, a convenient classification which, though not fully warranted in practice, was compendious and useful in theory. It was this trinity that stirred the worship of those foreign idealists who envied England's good fortune, and acclaimed in her Revolution a model to be followed by other lands.

Defoe was one of the few men of letters honoured by William's personal recognition. In the years after 1698 he devoted himself to the writing of books and pamphlets advocating what he knew to be the royal policy, namely, armed resistance to Louis; and, in 1701 he presented to an astonished House of Commons his Legion Memorial in which, claiming to speak on behalf of the nation, he demanded that England should stand by her allies. But his importance for this period rests on something more than these ephemeral productions. A Dissenter, he had been trained, not at one of the universities, but at a Dissenting Academy; an unsuccessful tradesman, with a large family, he had an experience of life such as was denied to all his eminent contemporaries. He was therefore a complete " outsider." As he fitted into none of the accepted categories, his attitude was individualist, expressed, not in the security and comfort of the study, but sometimes in the squalor of the prison or even within the restrictions of the pillory, circumstances which favoured an integrity of mind and a clarity of utterance denied to the majority of literary men. He experienced the solitude of one who is in disagreement with all the rest of the world and knows that he is right. This was linked with an imaginative faculty remarkable in the annals of literature; in consequence, he was essentially a rebel—not against the established State—but against something much more formidable, namely, an established mode of thought. For such a crusade a special technique was necessary. This was provided by his

oblique method of attack. He first disarmed his
opponents by appearing to agree with them, and then
so exaggerating their case as to make it obviously
ridiculous. There were dangers in this method, but
the weapons of sarcasm and irony may eventually
penetrate farther than direct assault. That assault
was waged, not on behalf of a class or a sect, but on
behalf of his fellow-men; accordingly, in an age of
exclusiveness and injustice, Defoe was the first exponent
of what is now called the " common man."

Practically everything against which he tilted was as
universally tolerated then as it is condemned to-day.
He was one of the first to protest against negro slavery,
against imprisonment for debt, against the iniquitous
" wrecking " on the south coast, whereby so many
seamen were murdered or left to drown. A more
respectable and more legitimate form of wrong-doing
which incurred his anathema was the practice, adopted
by some merchants, of sending unseaworthy, over-
insured ships to their fate. He showed similar im-
patience with those Justices, many of them vicious in
their private lives, who harshly penalised the pecca-
dilloes of the poor. His *Trueborn Englishman* (1701)
ridiculed popular dislike of foreigners, notably the
Dutch; later, his tracts on the Union of 1707 condemned both English contempt for the Scots, and
Scottish resentments against the English; already, in
1702, his *Shortest Way with the Dissenters*, by a supreme
stroke of irony, had reduced to an absurdity another
popular form of intolerance, by suggesting wholesale

extermination of Dissenters as a solution of the problem. Of even wider import was his attitude to crime, for he was the first Englishman to declare that crime has usually a social or economic background, and that a man may steal, not because he is desperately wicked, but because he is desperately hungry. Here was a revolution in thought comparable, in its significance, with the Revolution itself.

* 6 *

Conclusion

HOBBES PROPOUNDED the theory that the Sovereign takes upon himself the person of his subjects, but the philosopher lived long enough to see the reverse process, when, in the reign of Charles II, many of his subjects took upon themselves the irresponsible personality of their ruler. The English nation is specially susceptible to the example set by the Throne. This interaction is one of the most potent, though recondite influences in our history, recondite, because it transcends the normal human relationships, potent, because it is exercised with a degree of cogency second only to that of religious precept. Did England respond to the lead given by William and Mary?

In several respects, an obvious example was set by both. Mary was the first native-born Queen since Elizabeth, and so, as she had none of the remoteness of her foreign predecessors, her doings were followed with sympathetic interest by those of her subjects who had no Jacobite sympathies. Her piety attained, and even exceeded the most rigorous standards of her age, so that even her " Crownation " appeared to be mere vanity; her personal rule, in the difficult summers of 1690 and 1692, showed a Stuart decisiveness without Stuart capriciousness. Fond of music and gardening, she increased the popularity of these pursuits; as a collector of china and porcelain, she helped to establish the one institution through which women were soon to exercise their distinctive influence, namely, the drawing-room. Although Queen for barely five years, she exemplified a graceful femininity, unsoured by the tragedy of her childlessness, but saddened by enforced division of loyalty—though never of affection—between an unfortunate father and an unresponsive husband.

Together, the two set an example, not of conjugal felicity, nor even (so far as the King was concerned) of conjugal fidelity; but there was this change, that a mistress-in-chief was not installed in a position of eminence and responsibility. To that extent, at least, some respect was paid to the sanctity of the marriage tie and the integrity of family life; indeed, for the first time in a generation, these things ceased to be subjects of ridicule. But, in deeper ways, these two sovereigns had some influence on English civilisation. Mary had a quality not common at that time, and hitherto unusual in English queens—that of sympathy for others in distress—a sympathy which may have arisen from the acute and constant anxiety which she herself had to endure. This sympathy she extended to the sick and wounded sailors who, in some instances, were left to die in the streets, because accommodation in hospitals and lodgings was inadequate; so she ex-

pressed a wish that the old royal palace at Greenwich
might be rebuilt as a naval hospital. After her death
William honoured her memory by helping to fulfil this
wish; and so Greenwich Hospital, now a great naval
college, is the national memorial of a husband and wife,
of a wife who was stirred by a humanity still rare
among her contemporaries, and of a husband not
fully conscious of his affection until after her death.

For nearly two centuries the posthumous reputation
of William was very high. In the parliamentary
debates of the eighteenth century he was always
referred to in terms of veneration, for he was the
Deliverer who, having rescued England from the perils
of France and popery, had made possible that power,
wealth and freedom which were the constant boast of
Hanoverian statesmen. From backslidings towards the
altars of Baal he had directed the path of Englishmen
upwards to that Ark of the Covenant, known as the
British Constitution, a polity wherein toleration and
the rights of the subject were linked with privilege
and exclusiveness as nowhere else in the world. This
tradition lingered into the nineteenth century, when
historians and publicists showed a special interest in
Cromwell and William, both of them warriors in the
cause of Protestantism, respected and even feared by
Catholic Europe, each of them the embodiment of
that high sense of purpose and austerity of character
which the Victorians implicitly revered. But the
twentieth century, so tragic if only for its disillusion-
ments, is not impressed by that impulse of duty and

belief in progress which, in the past, were so closely linked with an ardent Protestantism; hence William, no longer revered as the product and defender of a great faith, has been displaced in popular esteem by monarchs of a very different mould. Nevertheless, although we can no longer appreciate William for the reasons which weighed with previous generations, we can now acclaim in him a great and unwearying protagonist against those evil forces in the world of which our own generation has had such experience.

In this respect William III has a European as much as an English significance. For the Continent, he appeared to have done little, since neither his military ability nor his resources were equal to those available for France, but he had proved that the course of the aggressor could be checked; and, at great cost in human life and treasure, he had preserved a barrier against wholesale conquest. Had he failed to do so, it is possible that the United Provinces, the Spanish Netherlands and a part of Germany would have been overrun or conquered by Louis XIV, and some kind of totalitarian empire might well have been established, an empire which, had the Stuarts remained on the throne, or had they regained it, would have included Great Britain and Ireland. The fact that this did not happen does not exclude it from the realm of possibility. For Europe, however, William meant something more than a conjecture, because he had saved England from the male Stuarts, and had presided over a constitution which, in its comparative enlightenment and stability, was the envy of the world. This was appreciated most by the subjects of his chief enemy; indeed, it is not fanciful to trace the more remote origins of the French Revolution to those popular songs which hinted that oppressed Frenchmen should follow the English example. That example was constantly held in view throughout the eighteenth century. The Deliverer and his Revolution embodied, for the apostles of the Enlightenment, the achievement of many of their aspirations; and so emancipation, brilliantly exemplified in Great Britain, was no longer a dream.

For his adopted country William did much. Not only did he confer on the Crown a new dignity and restraint, but he helped to promote the evolution of a nation. His personal qualities might well have stirred little but indifference in the minds of his subjects; nevertheless, he never aroused their contempt, and eventually he won their respect. His was one of the few reigns in which such a process can be seen, a process to be accounted for by the fact that so many of his subjects were sufficiently developed to appreciate in their ruler certain qualities either dormant or absent in themselves. They came to appreciate his loyalty to his word; his unsparing devotion to a great cause, his tolerance, his refusal to stoop to petty acts of vindictiveness or revenge; and from his example they were taught something which otherwise they could hardly have even imagined—that mercy may be proof, not of weakness, but of strength. His England, adolescent, divided and turbulent, had need of the example set by the public exercise of these, the deeper moral qualities; this was essentially an educative process, influencing men only gradually, and almost in spite of themselves. Such an unusual relationship was manifested most clearly in the last year of his life, when party distinction and religious difference were, for the time, thrust aside in the almost unanimous consensus of a people determined to face the threat from a dictator.

Of that tragic last year, when the King was wearing out his enfeebled frame in a desperate attempt to avert war, we have a memorial in a portrait, a reproduction of which is prefixed to this volume. It depicts, not a hero rushing, sword in hand, to victory, nor a general, standing in triumph against a background of carnage and conflagration, but the care-worn visage of a statesman who, having failed to achieve peace, was again obliged to undertake what must have seemed a hopeless defence. It is a face eloquent of despair and defeat. But he had organised the forces which were so speedily to bring victory for what appeared a losing cause. Here is the basis for the revaluation of a king. The England of 1702 was a greater, a more united and even a more humane nation than that of 1689; this is the measure of the achievement of William III.

Chronological Table

1650	4 Nov.	Birth of William at The Hague
1659		Commences study at the University of Leyden
1667		Admitted to the Council of State
1670		First visit to England
1672		Proclaimed Stadholder of Holland and Captain General of the United Provinces. Leads the Dutch defence against the French invasion. Murder of the brothers De Witt
1673		Captures Naarden and Bonn from the French
1674		Inconclusive battle with Condé at Seneff
1677	Oct.-Nov.	Second visit to England and marriage with Mary Stuart, elder daughter of James, Duke of York
1678		Conclusion of peace at Nimeguen
1688	July	Invited to invade England
	Nov.	Lands at Torbay
1689	Feb.	With Mary, accepts the Crown of England
	April	Coronation of William and Mary
1690	July	Defeats James at the Boyne
1692	July	Defeated at Steenkirk
1693	July	Defeated at Landen (Neerwinden)
1694	Dec.	Death of Mary
1695	July	William captures Namur
1696		Disclosure of Jacobite plot to assassinate him
1697		Conclusion of peace at Ryswick
1698	Oct.	Engages in First Partition Treaty
1700	March	Engages in Second Partition Treaty
1701		Renews a European alliance against France
1702	8 March	Death at Kensington

Bibliographical Note

Much of the present biography is based on the author's *England in the Reigns of James II and William III*, 1955. The fullest, and in many ways, the best account of William's reign is still that of Macaulay. Of this, the standard edition is that edited by T. F. Henderson, 6 vols., 1913-15. It should be supplemented by L. von Ranke, *A History of England Principally in the Seventeenth Century*, 6 vols., 1875, and by Sir C. H. Firth, *A Commentary on Macaulay's History of England*, 1938. Of books relating to William and his period, the following may be recommended:

G. J. RENIER, *William III*, 1932 and 1939.

MISS M. BOWEN, *William, Prince of Orange, up to his Twenty-Fourth Year*, 1928.

MISS M. C. TREVELYAN, *William of Orange and the Defence of Holland, 1672-4*, 1930.

G. M. TREVELYAN, *The English Revolution*, 1939.

MISS H. CHAPMAN, *Mary II, Queen of England*, 1953.